Introduction to Teaching with

OCT – – 2020

Zoom

Madison Salters

Introduction to Teaching with Zoom

A Practical Guide for:

» **Implementing Digital Education Strategies**

» **Creating Engaging Classroom Activities**

» **Building an Effective Online Learning Environment**

ULYSSES PRESS

Published in the United States by:
Ulysses Press
P.O. Box 3440
Berkeley, CA 94703
www.ulyssespress.com

ISBN: 978-1-64604-143-5

Printed in Canada by Marquis Book Printing
10 9 8 7 6 5 4 3 2 1

Acquisitions editor: Ashten Evans
Managing editor: Claire Chun
Editor: Pat Harris
Proofreader: Renee Rutledge
Front cover and interior design/layout: what!design @ whatweb.com
Cover illustration: © Freud/shutterstock.com

For Kristine, a wonderful teacher and a better friend,
and Jess, upon whose *acta sanctorum* I was able to complete this.

Contents

Part 1

Distance Learning

Digital Distance Learning and the Future of Teaching

The physical classroom space has been expanding for years to incorporate more and more technology as computers and applications become central to the lives of students and professionals, advancing us into the age of digital distance learning. As forbidding as this may seem at first glance, the scope of education has rarely been limited to the classroom: additional readings, homework assignments, hands-on activities, field trips, and out-of-school time that includes clubs, study groups, and after-school classes have long been essential supplementary pillars to well-rounded study. Distance learning, whether a replacement for classroom learning or a supplement to it, offers rich and varied opportunities that teachers may not have access to in a classroom setting.

Distance learning need not be viewed with apprehension. This book guides teachers, students, and parents in best practices for combining distance learning elements with the free video application tool Zoom. For you, the teacher, it will suffuse your syllabus with a broader range of learning methods and tools, whether you are teaching kindergartners or college students, whether your subject is math or music. Far from a crutch used only when school systems are hurting, distance learning via Zoom can make education more limitless than ever before.

One key benefit of distance learning is that, for the first time, teaching no longer need be restricted by time, place, or certain budgetary limitations. Whether you are using distance learning to enhance in-person education or as a fallback for use during snowstorms, pandemics, and utility disasters, it provides a rare space where you have tremendous control over how you present your curricula. Zoom teaching in particular gives instructors an opportunity to flex their creativity, crafting an online space that works best for their subject, driven by more individualized pacing based on their students. It offers better flexibility, originality, and immediate auxiliary resources, like PDFs and online libraries. With the correct road map, distance learning can be the place today's teachers go to forge the very future of learning—YOU will get to decide, in part, what that future looks like. You are on the frontier.

The first step in mastery is understanding exactly what distance learning is. To do that, let's contrast it with something the modern classroom is already a little more familiar with: online learning.

The Basics of Distance versus Online Learning

Elements of distance learning were already gaining traction before the COVID-19 pandemic plunged the globe into an emergent need for online classrooms. We can recognize the trend in the advent of online universities and the rising popularity of digitally taught college-level and continuing education courses. Unfortunately, this mode of education has often come with the unfair stigma of "lesser," even as enrollment has soared thanks to its accessibility, its flexibility, and, often, the lower costs of class materials. Technology is an undeniable fact of life, and distance learning has allowed nations across the globe to give students and young people access to an education in the midst of a pandemic, safeguarding them as well as staff and teachers during the worst of it. The trick to understanding how distance learning can be uniquely supplemental, parallel, or equal to in-person teaching is to understand the pros and cons of distance learning versus online learning, which teachers of K–12 students will be more used to. Online learning has its own set of tactics, which have to be modified or unlearned to approach proper distance learning.

You or your students likely have already been utilizing online learning. *Online learning* is categorized by the incorporation of technology into the physical classroom and the after-school space: anything from in-class tools like smart boards for teachers, school Wi-Fi, and school-loaned tablets or laptops to prerecorded lecture clips, digital notes and slide shows, school home pages and school-held social media to keep up with events and announcements, teacher email addresses, and even online resources for taking and grading tests and quizzes. Many schools, especially universities, use online forums like SPIRE to keep track of grades and allow students to submit homework digitally and access syllabi—something becoming more common in high schools as well. It's this high-fi/low-tech mishmash that categorizes online learning: education in a physical space, enhanced by technology.

Distance learning, by contrast, turns that idea completely on its head—it's purely technological learning, sometimes supplemented by the physical. It offers a completely new experience—think of it as its own genre. The classroom exists entirely in a digitized space, like the Zoom classroom, supported by a virtual library of tools and materials. In contrast to online learning, distance learning can be augmented with nondigital raw materials, such as books, snail-mailed packets (of bulk homework or graded essays, for example, for students who have less access to technology), and hands-on experiences like cooking, jogging, and physical note-taking.

Some other key differences include:

1. Strategy. Online learning treats technology as an auxiliary tool, an alternative style that can be used or discarded without much effect within the lesson. In distance learning, the digital tools are a must, and having everyone learn using the same set of tools will make your classroom more cohesive and collaborative. Proficiency in these tools is expected over time, and new tools may be added as they become available. Students will even learn how to suggest their own, and the addition of new tools will become common and organic in distance learning, whereas they are acquired less quickly and smoothly in online learning, and sometimes only the teacher need be proficient.

2. Collaborative studying. The in-person collaboration of online learning is usually limited to a few hand-raising questions and group work. However, studies show that age groups that work together on problems are more likely to come to correct conclusions and flex critical thinking skills. If done correctly, digital learning can be extremely collaborative. It employs video chats, breakout rooms, private messages, school and individual class message boards, and, often, the online individualized Learning Management System (LMS) of your school. It encourages discussion between peers at a much higher rate than an oft quiet classroom environment might, also encouraging after-class discussion at will—no longer restricted to just the class period or the school day or school environment.

This style of learning has many benefits, which you will discover as you grow used to the tactics discussed in these pages and become comfortable in your own Zoom classroom.

Some key benefits of distance learning include the following:

1. Relevant and relaxed learning. Technology is already such a vital part of students' out-of-school lives that they may feel more comfortable using a set of tools they are already immersed in, especially since computing will matter so much to their future professional and social lives. Distance learning will help integrate both application use and cloud-based ways of thinking and researching into their daily lives, making these activities feel like second nature to them. And whereas a classroom setting might be difficult and uncomfortable for some students—silent, stifling, requiring constant attention, and sometimes encouraging bullying—a digital learning environment allows students, in many cases, to pick a setting in which they are most comfortable learning and gives them the privacy to occasionally "goof off" in a way that may allow them to refocus. While cyberbullying can be problematic, in many cases students can more readily provide evidence in the form of screenshots and can work with parents and teachers to resolve it.

While not all students will have access to digital spaces and technology for learning (especially when students have multiple siblings, all learning digitally at the same time of day or using the same computer), in general, students will feel more comfortable at home, at libraries, or in places where they can use the restroom or grab a snack without disturbing the peace or needing permission. They can feel more confident and comfortable as an individual in a distance setting.

2. Enhanced motivation. Students who previously may have felt stifled by classroom curricula can be inspired by subject-specific distance learning methodologies that take their learning a step further by including them in the process. With less time devoted to travel to and from school and busywork, students have a greater opportunity to delve into supplementary course materials (tailoring how they'd like to learn and piquing their excitement for a subject) and to discuss lectures with their peers over videoconferences and group chats. With class activities like cooking or jogging at home, students are empowered by the idea that their out-of-school activities are an authentic and valid way of learning— learning is not restricted to time "in school." Students who participate in distance learning can be encouraged to take more of a front seat in their journey. The ability to review video lectures, ask questions when they think of them, and access lecture notes at any time will help them become better critical thinkers and more self-led, putting them less "on the clock" and encouraging lifelong learning.

3. Prerecording. At some schools, teachers will have the ability to prerecord some of their lectures and lessons. This can be of great help, since students will be able to access old lectures for review, and students (or teachers!) who fall ill will not be in danger of falling behind. The knowledge that lectures are recorded and presentations and class notes can be emailed, accessed online, or even snail-mailed will lead to students feeling more relaxed and attentive during lectures, being less focused on note-taking, and working at a style and pace that suits them. Prerecording can lead to better individualization of the learning process.

4. Time saving and place-flexible. While distance learning certainly cuts out the commutes, it also has other time-saving features. Online tests, quizzes, and homework questions that are multiple-choice can be automatically graded. Parents who don't understand elements of lessons or who want to help their kids can now go directly to prerecorded lessons. You do not need to take time off if you have a last-minute trip or emergency that puts you out of the school jurisdiction.

You aren't even restricted by travel time. You can collaborate with classes across the globe, even guest lecture in Beijing, China, at 5:00 p.m. after giving a lesson in Albuquerque, New Mexico, at 3:00 p.m.

5. Expanded accessibility. While it's certainly true that many districts and homes lack the proper setup for ideal distance learning—maybe there is uncertain, shared, or no Wi-Fi; no laptops, tablets, or smartphones; a lack of printers; the need for kids to share lesson time on the same computer; or homes where kids taking classes at the same time cannot get enough privacy from one another—this can be overcome by reforms that are slowly but surely being enacted with the recent focus on distance learning. Just as school buses, school lunches and breakfasts, and special education and ESL classes were adopted to help uplift education's most vulnerable, schools and governments are now looking at how they can better fund take-home tech, Wi-Fi hot spots, and more. If this can be implemented effectively, students who fall ill or who have a physical disability or mental illness can find their classes much more accessible than ever before. Students might not be restricted to education based on location, travel time, and funds to travel. If administered correctly and well, with an eye toward righting issues of social inequity, it can make education more merit based and equalizing, no longer restricting students to certain "zones" only, schooling based on tax dollars or zip codes. It can also limit the spread of illness. While parents worry that some tenets of school learning will be lost with distance learning, including child supervision while parents work and hot meals served by schools, many areas have already mobilized to address these issues. While distance learning, again, may not be a full-scale solution in anything short of a pandemic or disaster, for some students, elements of distance learning could make all the difference, even if classroom studies run concurrently. This accessibility idea expands into virtual field trips too, as explained in item 7 on this list.

6. Expanded control and creativity. Distance learning is all about personalization. It's your approach to education, unburdened; you are in control. It allows you to more heavily tailor to the individual interests and speed of your students. You can create a supporting study material library online, or, if needed, print free PDFs to send via mail. For the first time, this presents an unparalleled opportunity not to "teach to the test" (typically a thorn in educators' sides) but instead to shape curricula to match the organic learning environment of your class. You can even set up group-share classes with other schools and institutions worldwide, which for the first time makes it easy and free to do linguistic and cultural exchanges and virtual field trips.

7. Virtual field trips. A major dent in school budgets and a focus of fundraising is often school field trips, where districts, students, parents, and teachers face pressure to shell out or raise (by selling to those same districts) enough money to send kids on educational tours. Often limited by budget, those tours are generally restricted to the hyperlocal or are limited to the school's region. Museums and historical sites are often overcrowded, and keeping an eye on students can be a bit like herding cats. This issue is resolved by distance learning. Museums and culturally important sites worldwide have made their exhibits digital and their online tours free. Cultural societies hold free virtual lectures, talks, and question-and-answer sessions. In every subject, there are myriad "trips" students can take from the comfort of their own home, and they can engage with experts in those locations in a manner they wouldn't have access to even if they'd visited. Students can also engage in cultural exchanges with other schools in their own country or those abroad—like having a virtual pen pal or a language exchange buddy over Zoom, or working on cross-cultural projects of national and global importance (such as an environmental project on Earth Day). They can engage in problem-solving, enter competitions, and attend supplementary classes at other local schools with other local classes. Tutoring also no longer involves the time and cost of travel. Students can learn from experts and their regional and global peers, creating a closer-knit world by connecting cities, states, and countries.

There's no doubt that these strong points are helping to drive the popularity of distance learning. As it becomes more in demand, teachers who feel comfortable with these skills will become more highly sought after. Since the trend toward distance learning began in institutes of higher learning and continuing education, we already have some insights about its growing use and popularity to work with. Data and feedback from universities show that some of the most popular distance learning courses are in mass communication and technology—two genres that are heavily entwined with the online medium—but also, less obviously, in hospitality and law, which aren't as commonly linked to technology, computing, and online integration. It proves that students are willing to branch out, experiment, and craft a new distance learning narrative. If you are teaching children or young adults, this style of learning can help set them up for their digital future. Those who are teaching adults will already see the competitive advantage to this style of teaching, with so many remote and work-from-home options already in place and many companies already having international offices and workforces, often utilizing videoconferencing and collaborative platforms like Monday and Slack. This method of teaching gives them an edge and a head start in their careers.

Where online learning ends and distance learning begins has been a crash course for many teachers who were suddenly left in the lurch by COVID-19 and forced quickly into this new setting. They had to modify lesson plans and manage expectations, were suddenly interacting with parents on a more frequent level, became involved in their students' home lives, and had to become teachers not only of their own subjects but also of technology and distance learning itself. Teachers have met the challenge heroically, but it's time to arm them with better tools to do so, since the future of learning is changing.

And if the future of *learning* is changing, there's no doubt that distance learning will change the future of teaching as well.

What This Means for the Future of Teaching

The advent of the digital curriculum will undoubtedly have a profound impact on teaching, which can be summed up by the three P's: personalization, place, and purpose.

Personalization: Teachers of the future will collaborate differently with their students, having more flexible and personalized curricula and resource libraries based on fostering student strengths and bolstering weaknesses. Teachers will be able to provide students with more options for how to engage in the work of their subjects to best suit their style of learning, rather than a one-size-fits-most method. Teachers will also be supported by digital systems that they can customize to save valuable time—automatic test grading, prerecorded sessions, easy uploads to give students access to notes and presentations without printing out copies for the entire class, and a simple upload space where teachers can review students' work and refresh themselves on their progress, even if they have seen the work previously and have handed back a grade on a test or paper. For the first time, teachers can have a first-day to last-day folder of all a student's work throughout the year, NOT just a record of their grades, to help really assess them and recognize and highlight patterns. Digital personalization will allow teachers to maximize the time they spend doing the work most important to them, while minimizing the tedious.

Place: Next, the physical spaces of teaching will change. Because digital learning can take place anywhere, teachers and students need not even live in the same town. A student who transfers midyear may not have to leave their class. A teacher who has an emergency reason to travel might not have to waste vacation days. Most important, classrooms can collaborate with other classrooms, school districts, and learning institutions the world over without having to travel to them. Substitute teachers can also expand their district reach.

Purpose: Because engagement and teamwork are so important in distance learning, students will have the ability to be a lot more involved in the learning process than ever before. This can endow them with an enhanced sense of purpose and allow them to invest more time into pure learning—rather than some of the trappings of in-person schooling, such as getting from class to class, visiting lockers, handing in homework, or trying to borrow the same library book that 20 of their peers need for the same assignment. It will also provide an important lesson for them, going forward, on using, vetting, and assessing online resources for validity—for example, they can't just use Wikipedia as a citation; they have to look at the articles Wikipedia cites, read them, and decide if the sources are true, heavily biased, or false. This can make them better digital researchers, unlocking more of the world's research for them—an older student who has a commanding use of JSTOR, for example, can write topical essays with much more authority than one who is relying on physical sources near their location only. This grants, for them, a better ability to personalize their topics, and it can be vastly more exciting for them as a result.

Students' constant collaboration with instructors and their ability to pick and choose from an online resource library will give classes more depth of meaning, and in turn, having a more open-ended teaching system can allow teachers to feel more driven to try out new methodologies they are excited by. Teachers will be the pioneers on the forefront of this shift, knowing better than anyone how to format their classes to work best online. Teachers will gain a hard-earned captaincy in an even greater capacity than they had inside the classroom, to helm everything from how their classes take shape to how homework is submitted. And, as many teachers are already pointing out, distance learning often makes for better relationships between students and teachers. Teachers are finding that more and more, they're checking in digitally. Now they know their students' routines, more about their home life, more about other areas of their learning outside of their own subject or class. They know the technological aptitude and accessibility issues of each of their students, and they're learning whether voice, video, notes, or resources are the best way for them to learn. This knowledge can even be passed on to the teachers these students will graduate to in the next year, to give them a head start on effective lesson planning, so long as it does not upset any sensitive privacy issues.

One vital point to be highlighted here is that any of the tips in this book for distance learning can be incorporated into the online learning landscapes of your physical classrooms as well. Even if going fully digital for your school or students is not on the horizon, many of these changes can be implemented to make a meaningful difference inside the dedicated in-person classroom spaces. You can still launch Zoom from the overhead projector and host a language exchange with a student in Japan, for example.

The future of teaching will necessarily have to change to incorporate more technology because education is a tool to arm children for their future, and the worldwide jobs structure is changing to require technological savvy. The push for more workers with science, technology, engineering, and mathematics (STEM) backgrounds, more coders who know several digital languages, more editors who know Adobe and Microsoft and WordPress, more social media experts who know how to use analytics tools, more historians who can analyze artifacts digitally, and on and on, become par for the course. This change can be incredibly positive if integrated well and can help give students a head start for their actualized futures. The juggernaut of the pandemic has sped up what was a glacial shift before, albeit still a forward-moving one.

The future of teaching through technology can make classrooms more engaging, effective, and clear. It *must* be built with the most vulnerable in mind because schools cannot integrate distance learning until all students have access to the proper tools. It needs to elevate learning by being more inclusive, more engaging for young people, more creative in its execution, and individualized as a matter of course—all of which have largely been proven to be an aid to students.

Distance learning, its integration and understanding of it, can mean also that schools have effective planning in place for disasters and won't have to interrupt flow. Pandemics or even some weather issues won't have to interrupt student life. Distance learning can also be a way for students who require long-term absences, such as after surgeries, to still participate and be educated. It can mean that teachers no longer have to move to achieve certain jobs. A teacher who needs to be with elderly parents on the other side of the world will still be able to teach. It provides enhanced flexibility for students to work at a pace that makes sense for them; allows teachers to check students' work at their own pace *and* check back in on it; allows full-time access to course materials, including notes, lectures, and PDFs, that is equalized across students; allows for real-time collaborative work that can be tracked, through sites like Google Docs, for example; and builds a 24/7 learning community online for students to share. It will also require teachers to formulate new ways to make sure students don't fall behind: engaging in more one-on-one meetings and parent-teacher conferences via Zoom video calls, taking enhanced training to monitor for online bullying, and building a deck of outside resources that students can refer to for extra help are all a part of this new face of teaching.

We also must consider some of the hurdles of distance learning when it comes to the future of education, because it falls largely on teachers, school administrations, and local governments to mitigate the drawbacks. These challenges include the following:

- Students need to have the technology free and available to them. Schools and classrooms will have to find workarounds and funding to provide students with laptops, tablets, and Wi-Fi. As mentioned earlier, in some cases teachers may have to print out and mail lecture notes, tests, and essays to students with limited access or in low-income areas while federal mandates rush to catch up to this change. This cannot be emphasized enough as step one to effective full-scale distance learning.

- Students will need safe and quiet spaces to work, study, and do hands-on activities like science experiments and sports.

- Fighting cheating will become more difficult. New strategies will have to be implemented to cut down on cheating through the use of multiple devices. Some tips and tricks for this are discussed later in this book.

- Child care will need to be addressed. School administrators will have to think of how to accomplish distance learning apart from pandemic situations, when children are home from school but parents are not home from work.

These problems are often magnified for students of middle school age and younger, while students of high school age and older are typically more driven and responsible. Older students also have a more advanced comprehension of morals and ethics, and thus will have a greater understanding of both using technology in an ethical way and the impact of the consequences for not doing so.

Teachers in the creative arts and physical education may have to make the greatest shifts in their curricula—and they already have begun, via exciting, out-of-the-box ideas like table readings of theater scripts (have students on your Zoom call change their names to those of the characters!), virtual concerts, and workout diaries. Physical education is especially important when we are asking our students to engage in greater screen time, and creative skills will help refresh and re-center them. Creative use of distance learning paired with physical, hands-on activities that can be more easily implemented and supervised at home could also reengage our learners in some old-world subjects still of great use: shop, home economics, and, for older students, a love for play and "recess."

Distance learning can present certain extra challenges for students with learning disabilities and for special education teachers, but it can also be a great aid to students with disabilities, both physical and mental, allowing greater access to schools, more comfortable settings, and the empowering message that they are capable of using technology in the same way as their peers.

Distance teaching skills will soon be a set of talents that schools look for in their hiring processes. They are becoming an essential part of professional development. Therefore, having these skills handy, whether one is in the classroom trying to get a student to stop doodling or at home trying to get the Labradoodle to stop barking, will be an asset to any teacher going forward.

Distance Learning for All Grade Levels and Subjects

Which elements and uses of distance learning instructors should most focus on varies greatly, depending on the age of the students and what it is the instructors are teaching. The following sections offer helpful tips for teachers by grade and by subject.

Toddlers and Preschool

For this age bracket, the main concern is simply finding age-appropriate content. For this, resources like PBS's free online visual broadcast library can be a great help. Zoom calls for toddlers should be supervised by adults in the toddler's home or space, of course, but you can send parents music and videos to play for their child while you talk them through an activity or describe what they are seeing and hearing. The imagery on the screen will keep young children engaged, especially if it's colorful and if the video has fun noises. They can poke and prod at screens, especially touch screens, which makes for great play and gets them used to handling technology—so running classes on a tablet is suggested. Having parents download apps in which toddlers can doodle with their fingers along the surface of the tablet in art applications is a wonderful way to engage them with early technology. Have them proudly share their pictures, and wow them by putting them up on your own share screen.

For preschoolers, rely heavily on games. They sharpen many skills, both physical and mental, from hand-eye coordination to deductive reasoning, and they keep children engaged in the learning process. Keep the games simple: make very specific assignments that have one repetitive process, such as thinking of a favorite color and making a drawing using that color or thinking of objects that are that color. You can also assign physical activities, like jumping up and down. Make it a game by having the children hop once for every letter in their first name as you spell it out for them. Or have them do something funny, like bopping themselves on the nose each time you say "cat" while reading *The Cat in the Hat*. Getting them giggling and moving is key.

For slightly more academic activities, use songs. Songs can be played over Zoom using free resources like YouTube. You can learn songs to go with the alphabet, numbers, flowers, and animals—the sky is the limit. Songs that involve hand gestures that the children can mimic (like "Little Bunny Foo Foo") function well in keeping their attention.

Kindergarten and Elementary School

A wonderful tip for activity building for grades K–5 is to focus on current events. This can help students start to get used to using digital tools (such as search engines, navigating news websites, looking up sources, etc.) or physical ones (buying a newspaper, looking through a magazine, using safety scissors to cut out an article, etc.), either with or without parental help. Current events can build critical reading skills for older students in this bracket. For younger students, you can use videos on news websites or free-view sources like YouTube where news is narrated. It's best to focus on upbeat, nonpolitical news. By making it local, you can also engage students in their community, and some may even wish to engage with local websites and papers, submitting drawings, poetry, and letters. Or, if the news involves them in some way—say, a local community garden is opening—they can engage with it outright, visiting the garden, helping water plants, or planting their own flowers. With older students, you can have them do more critical presentations of the news, pretend to do newscasts themselves of made-up topics, or write short summaries of what they've read or what you've read to them. When they present to one another over Zoom, they retain more learning and feel more connected. This type of lesson will also make them feel more confident in their knowledge of their city and world.

For younger students, you can also encourage collaging. Have them cut out images they like from magazines (again, using safety scissors) and present their art over the video Zoom call. This will help them expand their creativity as well as their fine motor skills and will give you an opportunity to provide feel-good positive feedback.

You can do the same types of activities with specific cultural ideas, too. For example, have every student look up George Washington and learn one fact, dress up as him, or look at pictures of where he lived or fought the British. You can do the same type of activity with foreign languages: have children look up their favorite word in Spanish, for example, using Google Translate, which has the option to play back how the word is pronounced. This gives them a task that involves learning to use technology while giving the activity personalization, finishing with a sharing moment with the class.

You can also do a "groupings"-style activity. Show students a group of images and have them work together to sort them into categories to learn important skills. For example, if you're learning about nouns, have them place photos in the categories of person, place, or thing. Have the students sort and present them. They can learn more about those people, places, and objects as they sort them, and they can explain their reasons for sorting them as they chose to. For example, seeing a group of buildings and saying a building is a *thing* versus seeing a group of buildings and saying "That's New York, a *place*" can foster their cognitive development.

Middle School and High School

This age group needs a consistent push to stay focused and engaged in tasks. For these students especially, adjusting to a new teaching methodology might be difficult—they will be more used to technology but also will be more used to the physical space of the classroom. Make sure to suggest that they always work in the same space at home (or wherever they prefer or can learn) and that the space is set up as comfortably as possible for their learning, so they can feel like they are entering and exiting the study space. Even if their home or library space isn't large, they can carve out a corner, have a special cushion, or face their chair in a certain direction when it's "school time." It's about creating a sense of a space that says it's time for learning.

Using Zoom can help with another difficulty in this age group: keeping them focused and off their phones. While some students may naturally move to web browsers and new tabs or use chat windows during a lesson (the modern form of doodling), having students agree to keep their own video streams on, where possible, can cut back on this and create a sharper sense of community. You can also easily check for feedback this way: you can see who is alert, engaged, laughing, curious, and questioning and who might not be as focused. In classes that don't require students to have video feeds on or that are legally prohibited from having students on video (especially if the Zoom call is being recorded), you can pepper questions into the lesson and call on students by name to test their engagement level and remind them to stay alert, lest they be called on next. (This tactic is discussed in greater length in the next section as well as in the section titled "Translating Your Classroom to a Distance Learning Platform.")

Remember that especially with this age group, peer pressure is par for the course. Students might have additional stressors if they feel that their school life has been derailed, or if they're frustrated and feeling systemically cut down by not having the same accessibility, technological or space-wise, as their peers. This can especially be the case if they're in a home with a computer shared by multiple distance learners or are accessing Zoom via their phone, which may make accessing chats, links, and digital notes more difficult than a computer would. This is why it's strongly suggested that for older students, teachers record their lessons. That way, if students share a computer with siblings, they are not mandated to catch your lessons live—they can more easily share space and tech tools by checking in later to watch a lecture at their designated computer time or when an electronic device is available to them—some students may need or want to learn on specific days, in bulk. (You may need to be aware of this for homework purposes, so spacing homework out and being aware of individual students' situations is paramount.) This can greatly reduce the stress load for low-tech households and households with shared learning spaces and bandwidth. Also, because middle school and high school subjects are more advanced, prerecorded lessons can be helpful for learners who may want to re-watch explanations or who may struggle with the pace of distance learning. It allows students to read additional resources and then return to your lectures, enriching them. It may also be helpful for students whose families employ tutors, enabling the tutors to keep up with exactly what you are teaching.

Another major tip is to keep your personality in your teaching! Especially with this age group. Your lectures and lessons don't have to be boring, stilted, and droning. Be yourself—have a sense of humor, display your own flair for the creative, and choose activities that will amuse students, get them talking and debating, or get them competitive—in a friendly way, of course.

In this age bracket, it is also suggested that you have individual slide shows for lessons (using a free service, like Google Slides) in which you can share your screen and shuffle through slides as the lesson proceeds. You can still be live on camera, and you will still be able to see your class. After the lecture, you can include the slides in a lesson packet online.

Remember, high schoolers, who have so much going on in their lives and a huge course load, can be easily overwhelmed, especially by text-based assignments. Be sure to explain all homework, presentations, essays, and projects aloud to them and to field any questions over video chat after they've had time to read your write-up of any projects. This can clear up any confusion ahead of time and save you from having to reply to several long email threads, especially if many students have the same questions. You can even include links to short recordings of yourself explaining projects and homework assignments if doing so in class will take up too much time. This will make a world of difference. Make sure to include your expectations for the assignment, options for how to do it, and words of encouragement.

Vitally, take the time to provide personalized feedback. In the digital world, things can feel less personal than ever. The more detailed, constructive, and directional you can be, the better. Use tools like Track Changes in Microsoft Word and Suggesting in Google Docs to add comments and feedback to essays and assignments—make sure to say what you loved, along with what could be improved and how. The same can be done for digitized exams, especially those that are automatically graded—reaching out personally, and gently, to students who are struggling might give you a window into why they are having difficulty and how you can help. It will also bolster them, making them feel special and important.

Always make sure your students know you are there for them; encourage them to reach out and ask questions, especially if they are struggling.

Finally, make sure to suggest assignments that take advantage of the space of most remote learning: the home. Give kids assignments they might not be able to do in schools: safe experiments, safe cooking ideas, home improvement ideas, maybe even finance, accounting, or fun with physical education—such as making a mini at-home gym using water bottles for weights. Remember to modify these activities for all access levels. For example, if cooking is out for one of your students, have that student look up and source a recipe instead. Or see who can source the cheapest versus most expensive version of a recipe by pretend shopping online. This can be a great way to talk about economics. Get creative! And remember, individualization can relieve a lot of stress. In this form of learning, there's no one right way for everyone.

College, Technical School, and Continuing Education

For higher education learners, not very much about your lessons and lectures will need to change, beyond the medium of delivery and the vehicle for submission of tests, quizzes, essays, and homework. Hands-on activities will have to be switched to virtual ones in some cases, but for the most part, in working with adults and young adults you'll have some extra freedom in letting them know in advance what supplies and tools they will need to purchase and become acquainted with for your course.

For this age group, creating a sense of community and communication is vital. Be sure to have activities they can work on in breakout rooms in groups of two to three, and be sure to *pop into those breakout rooms* to help guide and facilitate discussions and provide positive feedback (for how to do this, see the "Frequently Asked Questions about Zoom" section). Give them something to do with their hands: activities to do on the spot (mute your own mic while they do these) for five to seven minutes, a couple of times each class, or more, if it's a longer workshop. Allow them to ask questions during this time, being present and engaged and ready to take yourself off mute if you have muted yourself for their group or individual work time.

Hands-on activities for these learners can be simple, even just using printed templates or doing a written task in their notebooks. Older learners will appreciate these more physical aspects. Encourage them to ask questions, and when you have specific questions for the group, make sure that at least 50 percent of the time you are addressing them to a person *by name* to prompt engagement—for other questions, leave them open-ended so chattier students don't become frustrated and can share their thoughts. Always be open to questions and interruptions to a degree (you can always tell students you'll have to reply to them later or move on from a discussion with them, but foster the idea that they can unmute at will). Asking questions of students by name will make the entire class feel more included, reminding them of your personal connection to them, and is also a great way to rope back in students who are losing focus and to remind students to pay attention, as they may be called upon next.

Be aware that older students, especially continuing education and professional development students, may try to find you on social media to connect with you after finishing your course. Have a strategy in place commensurate with your work code to handle this. If there is no harm in it and no legal ramification in regard to your workplace, this can be a great way to stay in touch, to include previous students who enjoyed working with you in future courses you may offer, and to solicit positive (and truthful) reviews of your work. They can also provide you with some helpful direct feedback.

Tips per Teaching Subject

In any and all subjects, take advantage of online resources! They are ever changing, ever updating, and ever improving, which makes them an exciting frontier. However, some steadfast go-to suggestions by subject are as follows.

History

For middle school through high school students, the Big History Project provides ample ideas for distance learning lessons for a single class, up to a full semester of content. You can even create your own online resource library for students to download and print. For younger children, have a look at Smithsonian's "Activities by Historic Era" (https://amhistory.si.edu/ourstory/activities/byhistoric.html) and formulate some fun and easy ideas around "Great Women of Our Pasts" (cutting out and coloring images is great for younger learners) or "Duke Ellington and Jazz" (a fun dance and learn activity for children of any age), for just a couple of examples.

Science

For science, K–5 learners can benefit greatly from the National Geographic Kids website, where they can play games to learn about the world and its many magnificent creatures. Many zoos host online Lunch and Learns, NASA has a plethora of downloadable content for all learning ages, and Science Kids (https://www.sciencekids.co.nz/) has a number of do-it-yourself experiments that can be enjoyed from home. For older students, the Stairway (https://www.stairwaylearning.com/) online platform dives into higher grade-level topics in biology and physics, and you can assign Daily Goals and hand out EXP (Experience Points) to help students feel like they're *Leveling Up!* in their learning. Free online science clubs like Oasis for STEM can promote out-of-class extracurricular learning.

Mathematics

For math, the online resource Prodigy has lessons designed for grades 1–8. CoolMath4Kids features a number of games that younger students can play, and MathScore brings to the table different adaptive ideas for all grade levels. Desmos provides free software that can help with upper-level learning concepts, from trigonometry to calculus.

English

There are book PDFs, free libraries, and subscriptions aplenty online. Many classics typically taught in schools are in the public domain and free to use. For writing, Read.Inquire.Write has a free online curriculum that teaches middle school students to formulate essay arguments. Young Writers holds several national writing competitions per year that you can challenge and encourage your students to take part in. A writing prompt of the week can also be an interesting way to engage students in best grammar and creativity practices, while a poem of the week (be it Shel Silverstein for young poets, all the way up to Yeats for the more advanced) can help students learn form, interpretation, metaphor, simile, and how to analyze text.

Foreign Languages

For foreign languages, teachers can find unique ways to incorporate apps like Duolingo and Memrise, which are learning resources for middle school learners and up that work on mobile phones and tablets. YouTube videos are also a great free, sharable resource, especially for younger learners, as young as pre-K. You can build a collaborative playlist of easy lessons and foreign-language songs for younger students, and for older students, subtitled interviews and documentaries are a go-to. Challenge them to watch an episode of a foreign-language show on a platform like YouTube or Netflix (paid), first with subtitles and then without them, for more organic learning. Or, feature a short free clip on YouTube, and have them write a transcript of translated subtitles! This can be a fun way to learn and interpret language.

Physical Education, Music, Art, and Other Extracurriculars

For subjects like physical education, music, art, and other extracurriculars, hands-on activities can be compatible with distance learning. Plan a yoga or dance class; have a sit-up competition; or explore art museums online and then set up drawing challenges based on the genre students have just seen and learned about. For music, watch virtual symphonies or musicals and assign sheet music by PDF—the existence of virtual concerts (hosted by bands and orchestras as great as national Philharmonics) and virtual media as on YouTube and TikTok means there is a market for this form of media, so kids don't have to feel their own online performances are worth less or "not real." Coaching staff can also use Zoom video chat to host virtual workout sessions with whole teams, accompanying them by phone on jogs, keeping times, seeing their reps, and encouraging and directing teams. Having team conference calls to go over workout progress is a great way of keeping up the camaraderie and team spirit of your athletes.

Special Education

Special education can provide its own difficulties in distance learning. For this, websites such as Accessibyte, which specializes in apps for blind and visually impaired learners, can play a vital role in helping students with disabilities. Whether the disability is auditory, visual, learning, or otherwise, a significant amount of free-access technology exists online and can be tailored to fit your individual students or classes through an array of apps specially designed for these learners. Teachers can integrate these into their distance teaching to help bolster their curricula. Some examples include AutismXpress, My Smart Hands, Learning Ally, and Ginger Page. Note that some of these apps may have paywalls, so you may have to adjust for what you, your school, or your students are comfortable with spending.

* * *

In each of these cases, teachers can take a page from university classes and courses that were already hosted online. The benchmark of these has long been prerecorded lectures, emailed lecture notes, online submission of assignments, and an accessible supplemental bibliography so students can work on their own and expand into the topics as they like. A great way to foster togetherness is by arranging smaller discussion groups over Zoom, with individualized questions or topics to address, or by hosting debates. Make sure that you also host online office hours on Zoom as a way of being accessible to your students.

These activities can be best supported by using Zoom to brief and debrief, provide feedback, conduct roundtables, learn apps together in real time, to share work, and, of course, to instruct.

Information for Teachers, Parents, and Students

Teaching via Zoom is something that inevitably will feel new—whether you've been doing it for only a few months now or were one of Zoom's one million users back in 2013. Because the Zoom platform has expanded so rapidly and significantly to support teachers globally, even the Zoom-savviest among us may have to get used to an entirely new set of tools and ways of thinking about distance learning and teaching via Zoom. With that in mind, the sections that follow provide information helpful to parents who have used Zoom only for work conferences, students who have used Zoom only to chat with friends, teachers who have been using Zoom for only half a year, and every person totally new to Zoom and distance learning right on up to those skilled in it already and looking to expand their repertoire. Being aware of the specific issues and questions facing parents, teachers, and students can also help set you off on the right foot on your distance learning journey.

Information for Teachers

There are a few things that teachers definitely need to be aware of when engaging in distance learning.

The first is safety—not just the safety of your students, in regard to keeping an eye out for online bullying over school chat platforms and even social media—but also your own safety.

Prerecording lessons can be of help to your students and can also allow you to script lessons in a way that is relaxed and assured. If you are giving live lessons, there is a chance of saying something that can be taken out of context. Be aware that your students can screen record your lessons on phones or take video clips of you, even if instructed not to. Teachers are only human—from time to time, we say something that parents could view as offensive. In the physical classroom, a snafu like letting a light curse word slip in frustration or humor is laughed off and forgotten in the next minute. On film, or overheard by a parent in the background, it can be immortalized. Many teachers say that they prefer to run their lines before going into a Zoom lesson. Another thing you can do, if you are not sharing your screen, is to read directly from set notes on a word-processing application, which will allow you say verbatim what it is you mean to impart. Don't get too stressed about messing up on a Zoom lesson—but do be self-aware of this major difference.

Another element of keeping safe is privatizing all of your personal social media accounts. While many teachers already do this, be aware that students are tremendously talented at digging up old accounts, old photos, and any unlocked material. For your own privacy, go ahead and lock it down—even if that means a trip back in time to the 1990s to add privacy settings to your old LiveJournal you've forgotten about.

Even though you might want to privatize your personal social media, *do* use your school's social media, or set up social media as a teacher. You can use this to tag and loop students into virtual events like concerts, museum lectures, author readings, art lessons, linguistic and cultural activities, and more. A tip for this is to turn commenting options off if you have an individual teacher's page, so students cannot argue, post anonymously, or be inappropriate on an unmonitored web page. For school pages, comments should be on and monitored for safety and anti-bullying.

Next, try to keep parents in the loop—have conversations with them. Teach them about the tools their children may be using and foster a good relationship. Often, distance learning implies at least one adult may need to be home or facilitating the learning process more than usual. Teachers find, more and more, that they are receiving questions from *parents* on how to open PDF documents, submit homework, and help their child set up Zoom. As this may be the group for which the switch to distance learning is the most baffling, be sure to have a resource packet ready to go for adults—including this book! Be sure to keep parents in the loop on major school dates and announcements, and lay out clear expectations for their children.

Just as with parents, try to keep up frequent communication over Zoom video and voice chat with your colleagues and administrators. It can be helpful to be on the same page about the direction of the general curriculum when the school is fragmented into different places; it can foster a sense of community, and you can share vital feedback and tips. You can even host small group events to unwind—a group movie or a coffee meet. You should feel encouraged to share lesson plans and go over any school news or shifts in local regulations and to feel supported by your community.

Finally, understand that distance learning, especially if undertaken abruptly, as in a pandemic, can be hugely destabilizing for some students. As much as your school can, make sure you are supporting them with school-distributed tablets, laptops, and Wi-Fi. Help families set up their internet connections, if you can. Be prepared to snail-mail assignments as a last-ditch effort if Wi-Fi proves impossible. Make sure your district is finding a way to still provide free lunches and breakfasts to those students who most need them. And, vitally, make sure students have access via Zoom to other important school community aspects, like school health professionals and guidance counseling.

Information for Parents

Parents need to be aware that the transition to distance learning may initially be rough for students who are used to the perks of a physical location, such as seeing their friends and engaging in club activities. To this end, creating a sense of normalcy is paramount for parents of distance learners. Try to make sure your students wake up on time, have their usual breakfast, and dress for school. If possible, have them create a physical "classroom space" in the home where they will go to work and that they can feel is different from the home space.

If you are a parent of a child learning at home, you will share the burden of the teaching job with their school. One important element of doing so effectively is being the disciplinarian, to a degree; make sure students are following a routine, and ensure they are reminded not to be distracted by other devices—TVs, phones, and so on—while learning. Of course, you are also busy, and it's important to set up the expectation that the fact that you are at home with a distance learner (if indeed you are) does not make it a free-for-all; you have a workday ahead of you, too. If you will not be at home with them, as in the example of a high school senior who may be expected to learn alone effectively, make sure they are aware of your expectation that they remain attentive and respectful during class and merit your trust in them. Be sure to follow up with them, where possible, about what major assignments they have due, tests they have to study for, and their progress in this.

A great tip for keeping kids on schedule is to produce that "bell ringing" feeling to help them parse their day and make them feel it's moving along. To do this, have your kids set timers to show when one class ends, when another begins, and when the school day starts and ends. They can do this on their phones, using free apps or simply the clock's alarm or time function (featured on many smartphones.)

Now, when kids aren't on school or homework time? Make sure to give them the freedom to just be themselves. Distance learning might prompt kids to feel stressed in the same way working from home or freelancing makes adults stressed: the feeling that there is no point at which you are "off," no point at which school stops. Create room for them to tune out and cool down.

Make sure parental controls are turned on for the devices students will be using, if this is a concern for you. Free sources, such as online libraries and video hosting websites, often make money through advertisements. To prevent your child from viewing anything you'd find offensive, head into the settings of the web browser on the unit they will be using for learning and make sure certain filters are set. You can also change your child's settings either to track what they view, if you plan to review their search history, or to not track what they are viewing, so that their data cannot be gathered. It is suggested in general, to foster trust, that insofar as possible you do not look into students' browser histories—but it is understood that this may not always be possible. Be aware, however, that many students will know how to clear their own browser histories.

You can augment your child's distance learning with an abundance of online and physical resources, most of which can already be accessed from home.

For toddlers and pre-K learners, you can supplement their learning days with plenty of song, dance, and even some kid-friendly meditation or yoga, found for free on sites like GoNoodle and YouTube. You can also find plenty of arts and crafts to let them get creative and work on their fine motor skills.

For elementary school students, focus on reading. Reading is one of the most useful tools for cognitive development, helps across all subjects, and is generally more effective in holding their interest than busywork. Reading is beneficial to the critical thinking skills they should most be focused on developing in this age bracket. You can find free online books through iBooks (for Apple users), Vooks (with a free trial, 30 days only), Starfall, and Epic! Take time to read together or discuss what they've read; this helps children feel positive about their reading, allows them to think about it more dynamically, and helps them retain information better. For mathematical and scientific skills, try puzzles, strategy games like chess and checkers, online coding games, and even cooking—have them do math with the ingredient amounts by giving them a recipe for a dozen cupcakes and having them reduce it to six cupcakes, cutting all of the amounts in half, for example. Or have them convert grams and milliliters into ounces and cups.

For middle schoolers, making the week diverse and interesting is essential. Switch up what you're working on day by day and give them more room to make their own suggestions. Make sure they're having Zoom calls with friends to chat and catch up and that they are getting a bit of exercise even if they haven't been assigned a physical education diary. You want them to socialize and siphon off energy at this age. Do fun cultural events, like watching foreign films or concerts together (live score movies are a winning idea!). Also help build their research skills by encouraging them to look for sources outside of what their teacher provides and to conduct their own original investigations at this age, using online sources. Have them explain why they think the sources they've chosen are valid and trustworthy.

For high schoolers, this is a stressful time. Of all students, they might be the most tech-savvy, yet they may be the least prepared for distance learning, especially considering the gamut of mandated tests and, often, college or job-finding requirements that they are up against. These students often have the most staggering in their scheduled subjects as well; some will take history, some will take AP European History, and some will be in Honors World History. Have these students learn outside of their online class. Assign them to pick a library book or magazine that they like in their subject (creative nonfiction reading can be very engaging). Encourage their writing skills with an online journal. Motivate them to also engage in skills they might not get to practice at school, such as painting, playing a lone sport, practicing an instrument, or stretching out their vocal cords. Make sure to check in on their emotions, too, to provide mental support for them. Get past the idea that they may fall behind on the gamut of mandates they face, and instead focus them on just the pure learning.

The best learning spaces for all age groups will be cozy spots (maybe toss in a pillow or blanket) with desks to work at, be they in a home office or at the kitchen table. If they are not using their phones to access Zoom, it's best to limit their phone usage to keep them productive. Make sure, however, they're getting breaks between Zoom lessons to refocus and reframe—they may need longer than they would to walk from class to class, but these moments should be more refreshing and centering than a backpack-laden sprint to class. Let them grab a glass of water, stretch, or take in some fresh air before following the new links or entering in the new meeting numbers on Zoom.

Finally, discuss what they learn over Zoom! Review the class materials; discuss lessons with them. Review their work, if you have time, or watch lectures together if they decide to re-watch them. Having live feedback, or someone to express their thoughts to as they learn, can focus them and give them more pride in what they're doing. Have them explain homework to you. And, if your child is more tech-savvy than you, as is more and more often the case, have them explain their digital classroom to you—like a virtual "meet the teacher" night. Let them, with pride, give you a tour around their new version of school.

Information for Students

The key to distance learning for the student is to keep yourself organized. A great way to do this is to input all important school dates and assignment due dates into a digital calendar connected to your email address or your mobile reminders once you've received the course syllabus. Set up digital alarms and prompts for yourself.

While using Zoom, liven up your day (and keep your living room or bedroom private) by setting up a fun or interesting background for yourself. This will ensure that your peers won't see where you are while you attend class—and backgrounds can be fun to customize. So long as the image is no more than 1,920 pixels maximum and 960 pixels minimum, is saved in GIF, 24-bit PNG, or JPG/JPEG format, and doesn't go above 5 MB in size, it will work. The best aspect ratio is 16:9 so that your image will not have borders or distortions. To create your background image, go to your Zoom Rooms account if you have one (note that this will change the background for all users on the account). In your Zoom web portal, click Room Management, then drop down to Zoom Rooms. From there, select Account Settings at the top. In your Account Profile table, select Background Image, then Upload New Image. Be certain your background isn't offensive, and poof! You can be distance learning from the Great Wall of China during your history lecture or from outer space for science. Backgrounds can also liven up and add humor to your in-class presentations, and because you may be the room host during study sessions (as opposed to your teacher), they can be especially fun and useful in these times. You can even email your teacher a background for them to approve and use during your presentations.

Remember when doing your assignments that often, once the cameras go off, so does the motivation to do work. Set aside a set number of hours per day, and try to use a consistent time frame, to get into the habit of working on your homework and projects. This is much easier to lose track of while distance learning, where the school day can bleed into at-home time almost as a matter of course, so go the extra mile to look at auxiliary online resources and be self-disciplined enough to get things in on time. It can be especially tempting to hand in homework late when under stress and when distance platforms don't close for submissions, allowing you to submit homework a week or two after the due date—try not to give in to the urge.

Check out and learn ahead of time how to use Zoom and the other online resources your teacher has told you you'll be using for distance learning. This will prevent embarrassing snafus and allow you to avoid wasting class time fumbling with settings, like not knowing how to take yourself off mute. On-the-fly tech learning can be really exasperating, especially if as a result you miss something important your teacher or peer is speaking about, or if you feel publicly embarrassed by making a mistake in front of the class (not a big deal, but it can feel that way). If your teacher hasn't provided a tech tutorial and/or learning how to use new tech doesn't feel organic to you, try looking up a tutorial on the technology's website or on YouTube. Or ask your teacher for guidance in setting up. You can also hop forward to Part 2 of this book for a step-by-step walk-through on how to set Zoom up yourself, including tips and tricks that can make the process and your distance learning more creative, fun, and intuitive!

The final point is to ask questions. It may seem even more daunting in tight time schedules if you have multiple Zoom classes in a row, and it might be more intimidating to have to come off mute while the teacher is speaking, but it's your right as a student to be inquisitive and to have your teacher help you understand the material completely. Ask, ask, ask!

Translating Your Classroom to a Distance Learning Platform

You can breathe a sigh of relief if you've been concerned that outcomes in education with distance learning might be worse than in traditional settings. Luckily, all research points to the contrary, the two can be equal, with the appropriate methodology and resources. One of the biggest deciding factors in how effective distance learning and teaching will be is how the classroom is set up, including, most vitally, how supportive the environment is to teacher and student interactions and how well it fosters student-to-*student* interactions.

There are some important issues to address that may negatively affect collaboration and energetic interaction in the distance classroom. Please keep these issues and mitigation strategies in mind when translating your classroom to Zoom and distance learning. Students may encounter any of the following.

1. Trouble feeling connected to you, the teacher. Students may feel in a distance setting that they are unable to ask questions as freely—maybe because there are prerecorded lectures, maybe because they've been asked to stay on mute, or maybe because they don't feel comfortable asking for extra help in front of the whole class. Be sure to schedule online office hours where students can pick a slot to have a videoconference with you one-on-one over Zoom, and, as much as possible, try to offer auxiliary videoconferences with help and tutorials as a group for any who need it regarding bigger assignments.

2. Trouble staying connected to peers within the classroom structure. While students may have no difficulty firing off a text to a friend or catching up later over a phone call or on social media, they may be feeling the loss of that organic connection to acquaintances and peers in class and, through it, opportunities for friendship and educational growth. It's imperative, therefore, to utilize Zoom's breakout rooms (discussed in Part 2) to their fullest, to put students in semiprivate groups to talk normally and work together, and even to assign work and study groups to meet over video chat outside of class time. You want to mitigate, as much as possible, students' feelings of isolation.

3. Trouble staying connected, period. Again, a huge problem with distance learning is that some students will have to learn "in bulk." Not all students have access to solid Wi-Fi, needed gadgetry, or, sometimes, even reliable electricity. It will not always be possible for students to escape to a café, a library, or a peer's house to have access to these things, especially in the kinds of crises that demand sudden distance learning, such as a pandemic. Be aware of which students have access and connectivity issues and try to mitigate them by assigning more bulk work (for those who have access only at certain times) or physical work (such as mailing assignments and including return address envelopes). Be aware that they might have different pressures in trying to fit a week's lesson into one day and may need different schedules for submitting assignments.

4. Trouble with direction and purpose. For many students, though distance learning broadens what is possible in education, losing access to the physical space of the school means their world has become smaller. Not having routine, set times, or, in some cases, even a certain future for extended distance learning, can mean that some students become unmotivated or gloomy or simply slip up. Make sure, therefore, that you're a motivational juggernaut, that you're giving clear, concise instructions, and that you're hammering home the importance of ethical and timely work, especially to their futures.

In setting up your distance classroom, be sure to begin the same way you would in a physical classroom: humanize it with a greeting and some short conversation, if not a morning meeting topic (discussed in Part 4). Build the space of your classroom vocally: share an interesting quote or daily fact about your subject. Then present your subject with the same verve and enthusiasm as ever—you have more creativity in this regard, and you *should* have to spend less time policing your class to stay quiet and keep their heads off their desks. To keep your students focused, ask questions often (and often ask someone to answer by name so you aren't met with the eerie silence of 25 muted microphones), and assign small tasks. If you teach an extremely long lecture, give a break, and encourage students to use the Zoom Room to chat during this break—encourage them also to use the chat function, especially to ask questions, which you can read and address during the break. The Zoom Room's version of "Settle down, everyone" is "Mics on mute, please." For some class types, cameras must remain off, and for others, having cameras on lends a great element of fun and ensures that your students are listening. Remind students that even if you haven't prerecorded a lecture, screen recording on their end is no more okay in distance learning than it was in school; and teachers, please do not do this either, as it is unethical and, in many places, illegal to film students.

To help translate your classroom, be clear about your expectations for the class in general and for each assignment. Be sure that all of your log-in details work ahead of time and that the links and join codes for Zoom and outside resources both work and have been sent ahead of time. Be sure that you and your students are aware of how to troubleshoot if something goes wrong (discussed in Part 2). If students' cameras must remain off during class, for safety or legal reasons, make sure to pepper in questions or to provide worksheets with questions students must answer and submit at the end of class. Provide these ahead of time to encourage focus during your lecture.

For disciplinary measures, if you're having a recurring issue with a student, reach out to their parents to have a videoconference about their progress—especially if they repeatedly lose attention or fail to submit assignments. However, with distance learning, positive reinforcement may prove far more effective: reach out to parents when their kids are doing especially well, to praise them, and let students know you plan to do so. This is an extremely appealing and motivating rewards system.

Send parents a guide for some of the simpler ways (even if you may think they already understand them) to help their student: explain to them how to open email attachments, how to save and send Word documents, and whatever else they may be curious about. You may find you're doing this more often than you expect, so save visual guides for future interactions with parents.

To help create the *peace* of your physical classroom, try to limit outside noise on your own end by shutting windows to block out traffic sounds, and create a quiet, well-lit space for yourself to video teach from. If your Wi-Fi is slow on a particular day and you are the one having trouble connecting, try restarting your router to help speed it back up.

The main thing to remember is that with good use of technology, distance learning can actually hold the potential for enhanced learning outcomes and better scholastic-student interactions. It allows for more individualized learning and pacing, and it's limited only by your imagination and daily goals.

Remember, above all—in your digital classroom, you are still the leader. Just go in with confidence and have fun. Be communicative and accessible. After class is over, hop on your school's forum to engage in online discussions with students and teachers. Be enthusiastic and they will be, too. You want to make learners feel that distance learning is actually helping to enable them, making them better students, not hindering either of you.

Using Zoom

Frequently Asked Questions about Zoom

As the instructor, you will be one of the most important resources students have in learning to use Zoom. Additionally, there may be paid and pro-account features for educators that instructors using Zoom have access to but students do not. Part 2 covers frequently asked questions by students that you may have to field, as well as some of teachers' most common questions, by going through the setup step-by-step.

Do My Students Need a Paid Zoom Account?

No, students do not need a paid account to engage in any extra features provided by their instructor—so long as the instructor has created and is hosting the room as the meeting host from a paid account.

Paid features include unlimited calls without interruptions to service, reporting access, and Zoom Cloud storage for recordings, whereas free group calls on Zoom are limited to about 40 minutes. These bonus features can be key to using Zoom as an educational tool, which your school ought to provide you with as an instructor.

In general, anyone may join and participate in a Zoom meeting without an account at all—however, for administrative purposes, encouraging your students to sign up can make all of your lives easier. Just be aware that Zoom does not allow individuals under the age of 16 to sign up, according to Zoom's Terms of Service. The outlier to this is that students under 16 years of age may sign up for Zoom as a School Subscriber, which is free of charge and explained in the list that follows.

How Do My Students Sign Up for a Zoom Account?

A free account can be made by visiting https://zoom.us/signup.

When you first visit Zoom's website to sign up, you will be asked to confirm your date of birth—this should be asked only the first time. If you are 16 or older, or if you are under 16 and signing up as a School Subscriber, follow this guide.

Via the website:

1. Open your web browser of choice.

2. Go to https://zoom.us/signup.

3. Input your email address, then click Sign Up.

4. Zoom will send an activation email to the email address you used to sign up. Open your email and click the button in the email or copy and paste the activation URL into your browser.

5. Fill in your first and last name. (NOTE: You may change the displayed name before joining a Zoom call, or you may do so during a call by hovering over your Zoom box and hitting "…" and then Rename. You may sometimes wish to do this if you are doing a play or presenting as a historical figure, for instance. But generally, teachers will always prefer your real, full name to be displayed. Do not change this without teacher permission, even for nicknames.)

6. Create a password.

7. You will be asked if you are signing up on behalf of a school—this is for instructors only, so don't worry about this option.

8. Click Continue, and you're all set!

9. Next, you will be prompted to download the Zoom app. You will now be able to launch the app and sign in.

For both iOS and Android mobile devices:

1. Open the Zoom app. (If you have not yet downloaded it, follow the instructions in the next section, "How Do I Download the Latest Version of Zoom?")

2. Tap on Sign Up, or choose Sign In if you already have an account.

3. Follow the instructions to sign up. You will need a valid email address to create an account.

4. Zoom will send an activation email to the email address you used to sign up. Open your email and click the button in the email, or copy and paste the activation URL into your browser.

5. You will be asked if you are signing up on behalf of a school—this is for instructors only, so don't worry about this option.

6. Click Continue, and you're all set!

7. Next, you will be prompted to download the Zoom app.

> a. If you already have it downloaded, launch the app and sign in.

> b. If you do not have enough space for the app or receive an error message, try unloading photos from your phone to create space, updating to the latest version (of your phone's operating system, found in Settings, or of the Zoom app itself), or uninstalling and reinstalling the app.

NOTE: Some computers and devices may require a user who has administrator permissions to download and/or install any new applications. Students may require a family member or other user with administrator permissions for the device to assist them in downloading or installing the app.

To learn more about updating or upgrading to the latest version of Zoom, go to https://support.zoom.us/hc/en-us/articles/201362233.

How Do I Download the Latest Version of Zoom?

In general, if you are wondering how to download the latest version of Zoom to a desktop, laptop, or tablet, follow this guide.

For a desktop:

1. Open your web browser of choice.

2. Visit the Zoom Download Center at https://zoom.us/download.

3. Click to download the Zoom Client for Meetings.

4. Save the download to your desktop.

5. Open ZoomInstaller.exe from your desktop.

6. Follow the instructions on your device to install the app.

For iOS devices, including iPhones and iPads:

1. Open the App Store app.

2. Search for Zoom.

3. Download the ZOOM Cloud Meetings app (https://apps.apple.com/us/app/id546505307) by tapping the Get button.

4. Follow the instructions on your device to download and install the app.

For Android devices, including smartphones and tablets:

1. Open the Google Play app.

2. Search for Zoom.

3. Download the ZOOM Cloud Meetings app (https://play.google.com/store/apps/details?id=us.zoom.videomeetings) by tapping the Install button.

4. Follow the instructions on your device to download and install the app.

How Do I Register for Zoom as a Teacher?

If your school administration hasn't provided an account signup for you or you're on your own as an educator, you can create a Zoom Basic account for free at https://zoom.us/signup. Follow the same instructions given earlier for students—only when asked if you are signing up on behalf of a school, select that box and add your school's email address. Once verified, you should be good to go!

NOTE: As mentioned earlier, group calls on Zoom are normally limited to about 40 minutes; a licensed Zoom account (e.g., a Pro, Business, or Education account) will allow unlimited calls without interruptions to service. Because of COVID-19, Zoom is currently lifting that 40-minute limit on Zoom Basic accounts that have a verified school email address attached to them. Therefore, if you are a lone educator (such as a tutor or an after-school educator for additional subjects), it is highly suggested you invest in one of these accounts.

How Do I Create a Meeting or Class?

You can schedule a meeting via the Zoom web portal. Once you're logged in, you'll see Schedule a Meeting in the upper-right corner of the webpage. You may also click Meetings in the left navigation pane to access your Meetings page and create a new meeting there. Fill out the meeting requirements and click Save.

A few important notes on the options available for scheduling a meeting:

1. Topic: This is the title of your meeting—you can name it the class that you are teaching and include your name, such as History—Ms./Mr. Teacher.

2. Description: This is optional and helpful for you to describe what the meeting is for. It will show up in emails that you send from Zoom to your students.

3. When: Select the time and date of your class meeting.

4. Duration: Select how long you would like the meeting to run—this is for scheduling purposes only and does not affect your ability to be in the meeting.

5. Recurring Meeting: Check this box if you would like this meeting to recur. Further settings expand when you select this option to determine the frequency and end date of its recurrence.

6. Registration: This determines whether you would like your students to register for the class beforehand—registration ensures that you will have a list of names of the students who join and participate in the class. (See the next section for more information.)

7. Meeting Password: You may require a meeting password as a security precaution, so that no one can accidentally stumble into your classroom.

8. Alternative Hosts: Input the email of your teaching assistant or whomever you might like to assign as a co-host in the event you are unable to attend your own class. He or she will have enough administrative power to make sure your class runs smoothly!

How Do I Record My Zoom Meeting?

To record your Zoom meeting, simply select Meeting Settings from your account, found on the left side of the page. Click the Recording tab at the top. You should see a toggle menu, and halfway down there is an option called Automatic Recording.

You and your students will be informed of a meeting being recorded by a screen display notifying you of it if you've joined by laptop or desktop. Those who've joined by phone will receive an audio prompt.

ONLY the host (the instructor) may record a meeting, unless the host grants this privilege to another attendee (a co-host, as discussed later).

How Do I Join a Zoom Call?

Teachers: Click your Meetings tab, find the meeting you created or scheduled, and click Start to launch your meeting room. This page is also where you will find the Meeting ID, if anyone asks for it.

Students: All you have to do is click the link sent to you via email. Alternatively, if you have the Meeting ID on hand, you can pop that into your Zoom app after tapping Join on mobile devices, clicking Join a Meeting on the Zoom home page, or visiting https://zoom.us/join.

Does the Web Browser Version Have Fewer Features?

Yes. The web browser version is limited in what it can handle—for example, you will not be able to see more than one video stream at a time, and screen sharing may be a bit laggy. Students using the web browser will not be able to participate in polls, and they will not be able to join a breakout room—you can get around this by keeping them in the main session and using that as a breakout room for folks who are running the web browser or who can't otherwise join one of the other rooms.

How Do I "See" My Students When Their Video Is Enabled?

Zoom has several viewing options, and it can seamlessly shift between them as you move your Zoom page around your computer. It is highly suggested that instructors use a laptop or desktop computer running the Zoom application for teaching rather than a tablet or phone, which will allow you less flexibility. You can decide to view your students in a checkerboard/gallery style or select Speaker View (which enlarges your own video feed while making your students' smaller). You can shift your students into a single, scrollable bar at the top, right, or left of your screen, which may be convenient if you are sharing your screen and need to view slides, or if you are reading from notes or a document and need a less crowded screen. You will still be able to shuffle through your students on these side or top bars, and anyone who is speaking will automatically have their feed (audio or visual) shuffled to the front. All images, both video and purely audio, will have a visible name in the corner of the feed.

For large classes, be aware that you will only be able to see up to 49 students. You can add and scroll through additional participants, but only the first 49 will have the option to turn their video feed on. There is no way to sort or put your students "in order" on Zoom. They will appear in randomized order, and then the order in which they speak, with the current speaker always appearing at the top of the line, and their own feed always visible as well. This is why it is of paramount importance for students to stay on mute when they are not asking or answering a question or presenting information. A giggle, a shuffle, or a sip of water can cause the feed to refocus on them if their mic is on. You can learn more at https://support.zoom.us/hc/en-us/articles/360000005883-Displaying-participants-in-gallery-view.

How and Why Should My Students Register for a Meeting or Class?

While not always strictly necessary, having students register to attend your class will allow perks that might be useful for certain lessons. One such perk is that it makes taking attendance easier, and another is that students' names are listed when you run polls—in nonregistered meetings, results may come in anonymously. Anonymous data can also be interesting and useful in class, so choose whether your lessons are better with or without registration. Other features reserved for registered meetings include the ability to manage attendees, resend confirmation emails, edit registration options (automatic versus manual approval), and edit your notification settings for the meetings, and you will be able to copy an invitation link to easily disseminate via the school's online, text-based group chat platforms.

Students who register will also automatically receive instructions about the meeting time and how to join the meeting. This does, however, put the onus of sign-up on the students rather than on the teacher to send out meeting links to the entire class list. So this method is best saved for when students are savvier and more confident with their distance learning timetables and use of Zoom.

To require registration, go to the Meetings page (https://zoom.us/meetings). Schedule a new meeting or select an existing meeting to add a registration requirement by selecting Registration: Required and clicking Save.

Help! I'm on Mute. Or Help! I'm Not on Video. Or Help! I Can't Get Myself Muted or off Video!

A common point of confusion when joining a Zoom meeting is that you might join and find you are unable to unmute yourself or get your image to come on-screen. To fix this, when joining Zoom, decide whether to give Zoom access to your mic and camera. On your desktop or laptop, you can do this by agreeing to it on the pop-up that appears; on your mobile device, go to Settings > Zoom and select Allow for the app to access your microphone and camera. And don't worry—Zoom will give you a preview of what you look like before you agree to enter any meeting.

If you are forced to use the Zoom web portal rather than the app (the browser version uses less bandwidth and is preferred for shaky Wi-Fi connectivity, and while it has less access to Zoom's features and may run slower, it also puts less stress on computers and some devices), make sure *ahead of joining* that your browser permissions are set to allow access to your camera and microphone. You should receive a pop-up on the right side of your browser tab that enables you to drop down and allow your settings to access microphone and camera. If you do not, try the following.

For Chrome:
Open Chrome and click the three dots in the upper-right corner. Select Settings > Privacy and Security > Site Settings > Camera and/or Microphone, and change your permissions. Then try reloading Zoom.

For Safari:
At the top of the screen, simply select Safari > Preferences > Websites and you will be able to adjust your preferences to allow camera and microphone access.

Once you are in Zoom, you should be able to adjust your camera and microphone settings by using the icons in the bottom-left corner for Mac, or in Profile > Settings > General listed vertically to the left on Windows, to adjust your audio and video settings. Or you can hover your mouse over your own image or Zoom box to quickly shuffle between being muted and unmuted, on video and off video. The microphone icon will also let you determine your *source* of audio: do you want it to be your headphones or your speakers?

Whenever possible, try to wear headphones to reduce feedback on your end when you are off mute, try not to set up your video feed with light fixtures or bright windows behind you (this will create backlighting and drown you out visually), and go on mute when you are listening to student presentations as another means of preventing distracting feedback noises. If students are not wearing headphones, you will have to insist they remain on mute except when they have a question or are called on to answer a query during the lecture.

As the meeting host, one tip for when you need your lecture to begin right away without any noisy preamble is to mute all participants upon entry. Students can unmute themselves, but this is a great way once the lecture begins to not let stragglers and latecomers disrupt the lecture. You can do this by selecting the Manage Participants option on the Zoom menu bar and clicking Mute on Entry, or to mute all students mid-class, you can choose Mute All.

For audio input, there are three options. You can call in using Internet Audio, which uses your Wi-Fi to connect to Zoom—please note, if your phone is not signed in to your Wi-Fi, it will eat through your mobile data plan to connect instead. Or you can select Dial In from your email link and the app will automatically input your Meeting ID. The final option is Call From My Phone, in which you input your phone number and Zoom calls you in. To use video on this mode, simply return to the app.

Can I Split My Screen So My Students Are Seeing My Shared Screen, but I Am Seeing My Students and Myself?

The answer is yes, but this gets a little complex, depending on your device and browser. Visit Zoom's Help Center at https://support.zoom.us/hc/en-us/articles/115004802843-Side-by-Side-Mode-for-ScreenSharing to learn more about this method, or see the later section titled "Screen Sharing, Student Grouping, and More Tips and Tricks" for more on-screen sharing. Using a split screen may be useful if you intend to share Google Slides or PowerPoint presentations.

How Do I End a Class Session?

To end your class, select the button on the right side of your individual Zoom box that says End Meeting, then select End Meeting for All. If you wish to let students talk among themselves after the lecture is finished, you can instead select Leave Meeting. (Be aware that if you do this, Zoom will select a randomized host from the remaining participants.) If you select this in error before the class is over, simply click Cancel.

When you end the Zoom meeting and exit, any automatic recording will stop, unless you have selected Leave Meeting. In that case, the recording will stop when the next host selects End Meeting for All or when all participants have exited.

Am I the Only Host of My Zoom Class?

The host of the class should always be the teacher. This occurs automatically when you send out the meeting links. Not only will the host have full permissions, but also, since as the host you are the most likely to have a paid account (Pro, Business, or Enterprise), your hosting will allow the meeting to utilize the maximum number of features possible. Students function as "attendees," which means they have the power only to enter and exit the meeting, mute and unmute themselves, switch their cameras on and off, and engage in the Zoom text chat if made available. As the host, you are able to fully start and stop the Zoom class, mute individual students or all students as a whole, stop individual student videos or all student videos, and remove students from the Zoom session. You are also able to assign a co-host, such as another faculty member, an administrator, a guest lecturer, or a student teacher. (There are an unlimited number of co-hosts, so assign at will and according to the user's importance to the lesson.) This person, or these people, will share your hosting license and can support while you teach, or vice versa.

NOTE: You can assign a co-host only once a class has begun, not before. The co-host cannot start a class. However, you may designate an alternative host while scheduling a meeting if the individual is another licensed user on the same account, such as another faculty member under the same school account, who will be able to start your class. Visit https://support.zoom.us/hc/en-us/articles/208220166-Alternative-Host to read more on alternative hosts. If you end your Zoom meeting without ending it for the entire class, a randomized co-host (or the sole co-host) should automatically become the host. If the co-host is a licensed Zoom user, the meeting can continue without a time limit, as with your own classes. However, it is better to pass along your host controls. For more on this based on your operating system, please visit https://support.zoom.us/hc/en-us/articles/201362573-Passing-host-controls-and-leaving-the-meeting.

Are There Additional Uses of Paid Zoom Features for Instructors That I Should Be Aware Of?

The answer is yes, absolutely. Since remote learning has transformed into a "new normal," Zoom provides a number of resources to bolster your teaching methods, such as screen sharing, student groupings, interactive breakout rooms, and more (the later section on-screen sharing and student grouping goes over this in more depth). This is discussed in more detail later in this chapter and in Part 3.

Setting Up Your Online Classroom and Lessons

When setting up to log in to Zoom to begin your school day, do some pre-class prep to get yourself properly "in the zone."

Remember to follow a lot of the same norms that the physical classroom would demand. Set up somewhere with good lighting, and make sure your microphone has clear audio (sometimes, certain shirt fabrics, jewelry, or hairstyles can brush against a mic and create distortion, which is something to be aware of, as you will likely be gesturing and shifting as you teach). Test your Wi-Fi connection (you can do this via Google or a free site like https://www.speedtest.net), and if your Wi-Fi is shaky, restart your router and try again. Dress appropriately for class. You will be on video, and you may be recorded, depending on your school's Zoom rules—you want to look every bit the professional you do when you are standing in front of your class in the school building.

If it is the start of the school year, be prepared to walk students through the school's code of conduct, including anti-cheating and anti-bullying rules—studies show that these reminders make a sizable impact on convincing students to remain ethical.

Because you do not necessarily have to be the first one in the Zoom call for it to begin, enter with your microphone switched off so that you do not disturb student communication and alarm and unsettle your class. Come off mute in a friendly manner, and then make sure to select Mute on Entry for any latecomers or students who enter after you. You should have already explained to students that they, like you, should enter Zoom classes on mute to avoid disruption, but they may forget or have technical difficulties.

Take attendance. If you didn't opt to have registered users, make sure to explain to students that they should enter Zoom calls with their first and last names visible (if they forget, they can change this by clicking on their own personal box in Zoom and updating their name during class). Otherwise, take roll call as you normally would.

Start with an activity or a small check-in chat (discussed further in Part 4), and then lay out the expectations for the day and the lesson's agenda. (At the end of the lesson, go over in depth any homework or upcoming assignments, and allow time for person-to-person questions; this is superior to emailing questions in helping students to comprehend assignments.)

Before entering your classroom space, decide also if you intend to:

1. Record the lesson. (If so, and you would like students to participate visually, make sure you or your school has written permission from parents, and allow students to switch off video if their parents have not approved it.)

2. Keep the Zoom chat feature on. You can control the chat's access settings and more from the More drop-down tab in the lower left of the chat. You can turn it off entirely if you feel it is becoming a distraction or if students are abusing it. However, it is typically a great spot to encourage students to drop questions that you can address at the end of class. If you want to address questions asked in chat but don't have the time, the More button also has an option to save the chat as a .txt file. You can then browse it later at your leisure and email students with an answer sheet.

Before you dive into teaching, decide also how you want to view your classroom. Do you plan to share your screen for some or all of the meeting? Do you intend to use split screens? Are you uncomfortable watching yourself talk, and would you prefer to not see your own feed? (You can hide your image from yourself by scrolling up to the three dots in the upper-right corner of your video screen or Zoom box and selecting Hide Self View in the drop-down menu.)

Determine how you plan to handle hand raising. When you are not calling on students directly by name, you can require that they raise their hand physically, and you can shuffle through the video feed and call on someone. Or you can have your students use Zoom's Raise Hand function—found if they click the Participants icon at the bottom of their Zoom box and select Raise Hand. To call on a student using this function, which is better for larger lectures, simply open the Participants list to see who has raised their hand and call on someone—it will sort students in the order that they raised their hands. The quicker they did it, the closer to the top they will be. This is explained further in Part 3.

If your class is getting rowdy or seems to be dropping off, remind them of proper Zoom class etiquette: ask them to mute their mics when not speaking, to make eye contact with the camera when they are, and to keep their video feeds on where possible and allowed, and require them to raise their hand if you're fielding open questions—but do encourage them to simply come off mute or engage with the text chat or wait for the end of class (it is up to your style) if they have a burning question of their own.

If you want to share files during class, do so either by linking to them in the chat box or by sharing your screen and later including those resources in shared lecture recordings, in emailed packets, or on the students' online school learning resource. For privacy reasons, Zoom no longer allows files to be shared directly in a meeting or chat.

Screen Sharing, Student Grouping, and More Tips and Tricks

Zoom has many features and a lot to learn, if you decide to invest more time into it. You can teach effectively even with just the most basic features—online talking and sharing— but tips like using screen shares, setting up breakout rooms, arranging polls, deciding on participant lists, and more can help enrich your distance classes. These tips will come in handy not just for teachers but for students as well.

How to Share Your Screen as a Student

Reminder: So long as you're still in the Zoom app and your video is on, your video will REMAIN on while you're sharing your screen, photos, and so forth, both on phone and on computer.

From a desktop computer:
> **1.** Click the green Share Screen button at the bottom of the Zoom window.

2. A window will come up that allows you to choose what you would like to share. The Basic tab's options include:

  a. Your entire computer screen.

  b. A whiteboard app that opens within Zoom, allowing for basic drawing and design.

  c. An iPhone or iPad, if one can be found connected to the same Wi-Fi network.

  d. Specific programs and/or windows that are open on your computer.

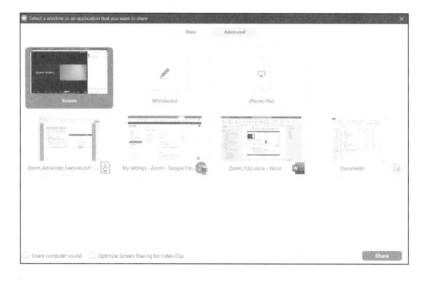

3. The Advanced tab's options include:

  a. Selecting just a portion of your screen to share.

  b. Sharing just the sound from your computer.

  c. Sharing content being recorded by a second camera connected to your computer, such as another webcam.

4. When you have shared your screen, these menu options will come up and follow you no matter what app you are using (i.e., if you move away from the Zoom app to show something else):

You will have the option to change your share with the green New Share button or to choose Pause Share while you're sharing.

5. When you are done sharing your screen, click the red Stop Share button.

From iOS devices:

Apple devices CAN share device audio but CANNOT annotate.

    1. Tap on the screen to bring up the Options toolbars frame.

    2. Tap the green Share Content button at the bottom of the screen.

    3. You have five or six sharing options to choose from:

a. Screen (requires iOS 11 or later and an up-to-date Zoom app): Shares your whole phone screen by using iOS's Screen Recording program. The screen share will include any texts or notifications that come through, so it's recommended that you mute notifications or put your phone on Do Not Disturb while you are sharing your screen.

b. Photos: Opens your photos to choose from—if you select more than one image, it will automatically create a small slide show, which you can swipe through.

c. iCloud Drive, Dropbox, or similar account: Opens your account if you connect to it through Zoom.

d. Website URL: Opens a mini web browser within Zoom.

e. Bookmark: Shares bookmarks made in the Zoom app.

f. Whiteboard (available on iPad only): Opens a mini whiteboard app within Zoom with basic drawing options.

4. When you are done sharing your screen, return to the Zoom app and tap the red Stop Share button, or tap on the upper-left corner of your screen on the red-highlighted clock feature from anywhere else you may be browsing or sharing on your phone. In other words, you do not have to actively click back to the app to stop sharing your screen if you do not wish to. NOTE: "Red-highlighted clock" refers to the typical clock telling you the time, seen on the upper left of your phone (unless otherwise set up to appear elsewhere). When the clock is highlighted in red, it means your screen is being recorded and, in the case of Zoom, shared. This is the same red highlight that would appear over your clock if you were to use the Record Screen function outside of Zoom.

NOTE: When sharing your screen, always select Zoom before tapping Start Broadcast—the prompt will display differently when your video is on (first screenshot) from when your video is off (second screenshot).

From Android devices:

Android CAN annotate but CANNOT share device audio.

1. Tap the screen to bring up the Options toolbars frame.

2. Tap the green Share button at the bottom of the screen.

3. You have five or six sharing options:

    a. Screen (requires Android 5.0 or later and an up-to-date Zoom app): Includes any texts or notifications that come through, so it's recommended that you mute notifications or put your phone on Do Not Disturb while you are sharing your screen.

        i. Tap Screen, then tap Start Now.

        ii. Zoom will continue to run in the background while you screen share. Choose any app you would like to share.

    b. Photos: Opens your photos to choose from—if you select more than one image, it will automatically create a small slide show, which you can swipe through.

    c. iCloud Drive, Dropbox, or similar account: Opens your account if you connect to it through Zoom.

    d. Website URL: Opens a mini web browser within Zoom.

    e. Bookmark: Shares bookmarks made in the Zoom app.

    f. Whiteboard: Opens a mini whiteboard app within Zoom with basic drawing options.

4. When you are done sharing your screen, return to the Zoom app and tap the red Stop Share button.

How to Share Your Screen as a Teacher, and Other Useful Tips and Tricks

See the earlier section titled "How to Share Your Screen as a Student" for the basic how-to steps. This section illustrates a few administrator-specific abilities. There are additional options available for the host of the meeting, allowing different sharing preferences.

Meeting Options for the Host

1. Security: Allows the host to lock the meeting, enable a waiting room, and determine who can share their screen, whether the chat function is allowed, whether users can rename themselves, and whether users can unmute themselves. Also allows the host to remove or report participants.

2. Participants: Brings up the Participants window, which shows a list of all the people who have joined the call and all the actions the meeting host may take regarding them, including muting all participants. Hovering over each name also brings up actions on individual participants, such as Mute/Ask to Unmute and Ask to Start/Stop Video.

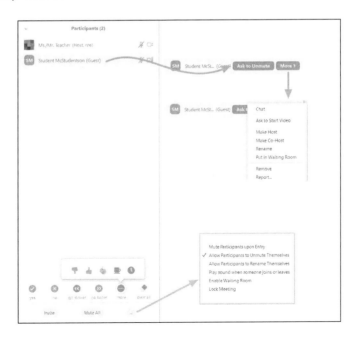

Advanced tip: This window also allows all participants to provide nonverbal feedback (different from reactions, described in the list that follows) such as yes and no, which displays as a small icon next to their name. This could be useful for giving nonverbal feedback during a student's presentation or for conducting impromptu polls without creating an official poll (counts for each vote are marked above the option at the bottom of the window).

Students will also be able to raise a virtual hand, which will display an icon by their name in the Participants window (or a notification will pop up above the menu at the bottom of the screen if you do not have that window open), as well as one in the upper-left corner of their video feed (as with reactions).

3. Polls: This option appears only if your scheduled meeting has a poll already available—you will have to create the poll in advance of your meeting on your

Meetings page (https://zoom.us/meeting). You may toggle between polls at will. Please see the later section on polls page 62 for more detailed information.

4. Chat: Brings up a rudimentary chat function that allows participants to chat with one another, whether with a specific person or with everyone in the meeting. Settings may be adjusted to allow participants to chat with no one, only the host, everyone publicly, and everyone publicly and privately.

5. Additional Share Screen Features: Sharing the screen was described in detail in the previous sections on how to share your screen as a student, but hosts (typically the instructor) will have more options available to them, such as adjusting sharing options by clicking the arrow next to the Share Screen button, as well as being able to launch polls and annotating on the screen-sharing menu (if enabled).

6. Record: Offers the options to record the meeting directly to your computer as a video file or to the cloud on the web version of Zoom. It's recommended to record to the cloud in order to also receive an automatically transcribed version of the recording.

7. Breakout Rooms: Brings up the control panel for creating breakout rooms, splitting the group of participants up into smaller groups for more intimate discussions. See the "Breakout Rooms" section on page 69 for more information on how to set these up.

8. Reactions: Shows a thumbs-up or clapping emoji in the upper-left corner of your video feed for a brief time as a nonverbal reaction. Useful for when you are on mute or don't want to interrupt someone who's speaking while still expressing your approval.

Starting and Stopping a Student's Video

As with muting and unmuting students, you may request that students start or stop their videos. Simply hover over the student's name on the Participant list and use the More option to find the action.

Here is what the notifications may look like on the students' end if you request or enforce these actions.

Desktop notifications:

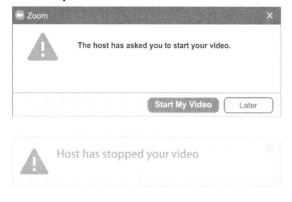

Mobile (iOS) notifications:

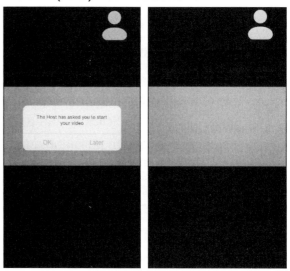

Polls

NOTE: Participants' names will come up only if they joined the meeting as a registered participant or if they have a Zoom account. Otherwise, they will simply be referred to as Guest in the poll results.

To enable polling on your account:

1. Open your web browser.

2. Go to your settings (https://zoom.us/profile/setting).

3. Click the Meeting tab to open your meeting settings.

4. Click or scroll to the In Meeting (Basic) section, and scroll down until you find the Polling option.

5. Ensure that the setting is toggled on. If it is disabled, click to enable it.

6. Your settings should automatically save.

7. Now that polling is enabled, you may add polls to your meetings.

NOTE: Polls must be added prior to the meeting in order for the option to present a poll to appear in the menu during your meeting.

To create or edit a poll before your class:

1. Open your web browser.

2. Go to your Meetings setting (https://zoom.us/meeting).

3. Click the Upcoming Meetings tab.

4. Schedule a new meeting or click on the meeting that you would like to add a poll to.

5. Scroll to the bottom of the Meetings page to find the section for polls.

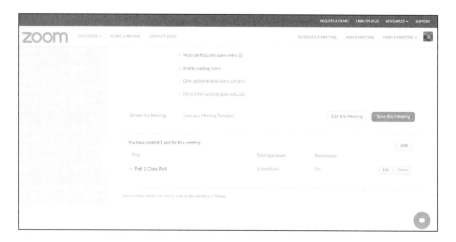

6. Click the Add button to create a new poll. NOTE: You may create a maximum of 25 polls for a single meeting.

> a. You may make the poll anonymous by checking the Anonymous box.

> b. Reminder: For non-anonymous polls, participants' names will come up as Guest if they have not registered for the meeting or for a Zoom account.

7. Enter a title for the poll. This will be visible to your students when you present the poll.

8. Type a question and at least two answers.

9. Select whether you would like the question to allow only one choice or multiple choices.

10. Click "+ Add a Question" if you would like to add additional questions to that poll.

11. Repeat until you are done.

12. Click Save at the bottom when you are done.

When you launch a poll, Zoom will allow attendees to see the poll you've selected, and it will begin a timer in the upper-right corner to display how long the poll is live.

To launch a poll during your class:

1. Start the Zoom meeting that you have added the poll to.

2. Click the Polls option on your menu bar.

3. If you have more than one poll for the meeting, select the poll you would like to launch.

4. Click the Launch Polling button.

5. Participants will be prompted to complete the polling questions, much as with a survey. You will be able to see the results in real time as they come in.

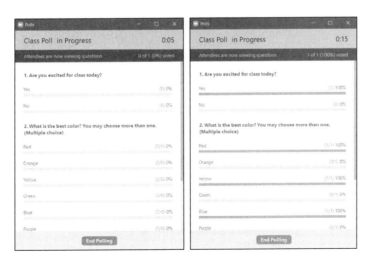

6. When you are ready to stop the poll, click End Polling. This will close the poll and show you the results.

7. If you would like to share the poll results with the participants during the meeting, click Share Results.

8. If you relaunch the poll, you will erase all previously collected results. You will be given a warning regarding this before you relaunch.

Introduction to Teaching with **Zoom**

After the meeting has concluded, you may want to download a report of the results. If registration was turned on, the participants' names and email addresses will be listed—otherwise, it will show results but list users as guests.

To download poll results:

1. Open your web browser.

2. Go to your Usage Reports page (https://zoom.us/account/report). NOTE: This is available only for Pro accounts at this time.

3. Click Meeting to view the registration and poll reports.

4. Select Poll Report as the report type and the time range you would like to search for your meeting and/or when you started the poll.

5. Click Search.

6. Click Generate next to the poll that you would like to see the results for.

7. When the report is done processing, click Download to download a CSV file of your poll results. (Files in CSV format—the acronym stands for "comma-separated values"—are used to move data between applications such as spreadsheets.)

Creating a Waiting Room

Waiting rooms can be useful if you want to have the meeting empty when you enter it and then select when you want to let your students enter. It can feel a bit like leaving your classroom door closed until everyone is lined up outside and ready to come in and begin their lessons, which can give your students a feeling of order rather than the chaos of showing up in an empty room. Here's a quick how-to to set up waiting rooms for your class.

1. Open your web browser.

2. Go to your Settings (to do this, sign into your Zoom portal, and in the navigation panel go to Account Management > Account Settings).

3. Click In Meeting (Advanced), and then scroll down until you find the "Waiting room" option.

4. Ensure that the setting is toggled on. If it is disabled, click to enable it.

5. Choose which participants to automatically place in the waiting room: everyone, users not using your school account, or users who are not in your account and not part of your whitelisted domains. (It's recommended to put everyone in the waiting room to prevent chaos!)

6. You may also customize the title, logo, and description presented to participants when they join the waiting room.

7. Your settings should automatically save.

Breakout Rooms

Breakout rooms will be one of the most important functions of your Zoom Pro as an educator, both in creating a sense of community and in encouraging student participation. In breakout rooms, students can engage in dialogue and debate and can work on projects and riddle out assignments together. This is a key element for creating fun and engagement, making elements of the lecture stick, and getting students to work together and refocus, especially during long lectures. It is suggested that you attempt to utilize breakout rooms *at least* once and up to three times per lesson. Breakout rooms take a little extra time than group work in a live, in-person setting might, so tack on two minutes to any assignment as a rule of thumb. If you think an assignment would typically take five minutes, give students seven. This gives them more wiggle room, as they might be slow to enter their breakout rooms or might be working with a student who is new to them and may wish to introduce themselves.

Breakout rooms are often the best part of class for students, and you can improve the overall utility of the rooms by popping into them to provide help, insight, guidance, and encouragement and to make sure students know to stay on track (lest the teacher appear from the void!). This is proven to help students stay on topic and to bolster them in their engagement with the material. Allow at least one group to present their findings or conclusions after group work, to give breakout rooms a sense of worth.

You can create up to fifty separate breakout rooms, with a maximum of 200 participants per room (which you can increase if you speak with your account administrator if necessary). In each breakout room, participants will have full audio, video, and screen-share capabilities.

If you are recording the meeting to the cloud, note that your recording will cover only the main room, even if you as the host enter one of the breakout rooms. However, if you are recording the meeting to your computer, Zoom will record whichever room the person recording is in—and multiple people (e.g., your co-hosts) can record locally at one time.

NOTE: Participants who join via the Zoom web portal, Zoom Rooms (conference rooms, not likely to come up for students), or 323/SIP Room Connector devices will not be able to join breakout rooms—the main room may be used as an alternative session for these users. (For those of you new to the 323/SIP Room Connector, this device, also known as a "Zoom Connector," can be purchased through Zoom at https://zoom.us/roomconnector, and allows you to share Zoom calls across devices/screens for advanced connectivity. Many teachers will not need this, but administrative teams may wish to look into it for its wireless and cloud capabilities. In general, however, this is more likely to be used in a corporate setting.)

To enable breakout rooms on your account:

1. Open your web browser.

2. Go to your Settings (https://zoom.us/profile/setting).

3. Click the Meeting tab to open your meeting settings.

4. Click In Meeting (Advanced), or scroll down until you find the Breakout Room option.

5. Ensure that the setting is toggled on. If it is disabled, click to enable it. If you wish, you may also allow the host to assign participants to breakout rooms in advance of the meeting. If you choose this option, remember to click Save!

6. Your settings should automatically save.

To create breakout rooms:

1. Start your scheduled meeting.

2. Click Breakout Rooms on the menu bar at the bottom of your screen.

3. Select the number of rooms you would like to create, and indicate whether you want your students to be sorted into the rooms automatically or manually.

a. The Automatically option lets Zoom split all students evenly into the rooms, with the option to move students manually between rooms as necessary.

b. The Manually option allows you to manually assign all students to rooms.

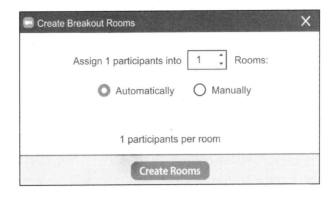

4. Click Create Rooms—this will create them but will not begin them.

To assign students to breakout rooms:

1. For manual assignments, click Assign next to the breakout room you would like to begin assigning students to. Repeat this for each room until all students have been assigned to a room. Participants who have not been assigned to a room will remain in the main session when the rooms are started. The number of participants will show in place of the Assign button.

2. For automatic assignments, students will be split evenly across all of the breakout rooms. You may manually manage and reassign them as you see fit by hovering over a student's name and clicking "Move to" or Exchange to swap with another student.

What can I do to/in a breakout room?

Some of the usefulness of breakout rooms can really be understood only by seeing the ways in which educators and students can use them. To this end, it's important to note that educators can create, delete, and rename breakout rooms; change settings, such as put a time limit on the rooms; and assign, move, and exchange students into and out of each room BEFORE starting the breakout session. This allows you, as a teacher, complete power and flexibility over the rooms, to make them work for the exact sizing and timing you are hoping for. You can jump into breakout rooms to check up on students (suggested), or give them some time to discuss in full privacy (also sometimes very useful). Additional options and settings you can select include, among others, how long the breakout room will last, who will pair with whom in what groups and what group sizes, and whether you would like a 60-second countdown timer to inform students when they're going to be returned to the main meeting room and full group. If you want to reset the breakout rooms, you may click Recreate Rooms to delete all existing breakout rooms and start from scratch. You may also keep some students from entering breakout rooms by not sending them the invitation link, if, for instance, they need extra help and you'd prefer to work with them yourself for the duration.

When you're ready to open the breakout session, click Open All Rooms to start. All participants will receive a prompt asking them to join their respective breakout rooms, while you (the host) will remain in the main meeting. Any participants who have not joined the breakout session will have Not Joined displayed next to their name and will remain in the main meeting with you.

How do I make an announcement to all of my students while they're in their breakout rooms?

You can broadcast a message to all of the rooms by clicking "Broadcast a message to all"—simply type your message and hit Broadcast. All rooms and participants will see your message pop up on their screens.

Can I check in on my students in their breakout rooms?

Yes! You can manually join the room by clicking Join next to the breakout room you'd like to enter, as well as leave to return to the main meeting at will.

What if my students need me? Do they have to come back to the main room to get my attention?

Students can ask for help by clicking the Ask for Help button in their breakout rooms. You will receive a pop-up notification showing who requested help and which room they're in. You can click Join Breakout Room to join the room immediately, or you can dismiss the notification and manually join.

How do I close the breakout session?

Click Close All Rooms, which will close all rooms after a 60-second countdown and automatically return everyone to the main meeting. You may also set a timer for the length of time you would like the breakout session to last under the Options drop-down menu; do this when you're creating the breakdown rooms or before starting the session.

Annotation

A final tip is that you, as the host, are able to annotate while sharing your screen. You can type on it, draw, circle, even add clip art, just as you would with a smart board. (You can also extend this permission to students if you so wish.) This is an amazing way to get your students to collaborate with you, and it holds their interest and cheers them up mid-lecture. You are also able, in this capacity, to share a virtual whiteboard.

For detailed instructions according to your device, visit https://support.zoom.us/hc/en-us/articles/115005706806-Using-annotation-tools-on-a-shared-screen-or-whiteboard.

Troubleshooting

Zoom, like all technology, has fallible moments. In these moments, we can tend to want to pull our own hair out—but don't fret! You have a ton of support options.

One of the trickiest Zoom options is attempting to use it via a web browser rather than the app, in order to save on Wi-Fi bandwidth. This often causes errors.

How to Use Zoom in Your Web Browser

Students who open Zoom using only their web browser should follow these instructions:

1. Open Zoom in your web browser by going to https://zoom.us, signing in, and then going to https://zoom.us/join to join a meeting.

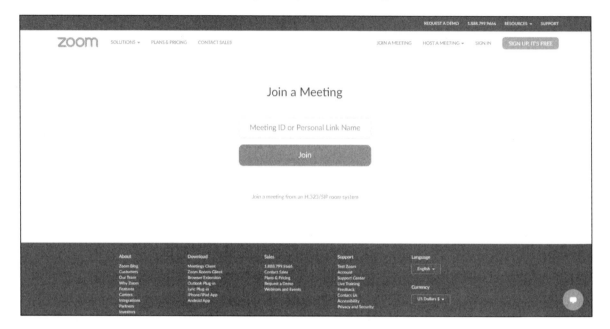

2. Type in the Meeting ID provided by your teacher.

3. Click Join.

4. You may be asked to turn permissions on for Zoom to access your camera and microphone in order to participate in the class. (Another way to do this is by simply following the Zoom meeting link your instructor emailed you prior to the class. In the popup that appears, you should have the option to load the meeting in your web browser rather than through the app.)

Notes:

- You will find the Meeting ID on your Meetings page.

- If students have to join by web browser, be sure that they turn permissions on for Zoom and their web browser to access their camera and microphone.

Introduction to Teaching with **Zoom**

- Some functions, such as breakout rooms, are not supported by the web-only version of Zoom. For students using this option, leave them in the main meeting session and treat that as an additional breakout room (for more information, see the section on breakout rooms).

How to Update Your Zoom App

To learn more about updating or upgrading to the latest version of Zoom, go to https://support.zoom.us/hc/en-us/articles/201362233.

Desktop client:

1. Open your desktop client.

2. On the dashboard window, click on your profile picture in the upper-right-hand corner.

3. Click Check for Updates.

4. If a newer version is available, you will be prompted to download and install new updates.

You can also update Zoom by redownloading and reinstalling it on your desktop. Simply:

1. Open your web browser and go to the Zoom home page: https://zoom.us.

2. Hover over Resources in the upper-right-hand corner, then click Download Zoom Client to open the downloads page.

3. Click the Download button for Zoom Client for Meetings for the most up-to-date version of Zoom.

4. When the download is complete, open the installation program and follow the instructions to install Zoom to your computer.

This method can be especially useful if you are operating Zoom on an Apple product, as updates can sometimes scramble certain features and lead to bugs or lags. Redownloading and reinstalling with new updates, as opposed to simply updating via the Zoom client, can avoid those issues.

Updating the mobile app (iOS and Android):

1. You will receive a mobile notification on the app if a new version of Zoom is available for download.

2. Follow your phone's instructions to update your app.

Other Zoom Issues

Most issues with Zoom can be resolved by trying the following:

- Restart your device.

- Turn Airplane Mode (found in Settings) on and then off on your mobile device to "reset" its Wi-Fi and data. (Make sure Wi-Fi is also turned off when you do this.)

- Restart your internet router, especially if it fails a free online speed test.

- Turn Wi-Fi off and back on again on your computer or tablet.

- Update your device.

- Update to the latest version of Zoom.

- Uninstall Zoom, throwing out the old version of the app on your computer (or nixing the app on your phone), and then reinstall it. This will solve most update problems with your device or Zoom's compatibility.

- Restart the app.

If you are having audio or visual issues with Zoom, enter the application to join your class, then play with the individual audio and visual options using the microphone and camera settings. The app may have switched jacks on you (say, from the headphones you're using to the Bluetooth device lounging in your kitchen); if so, simply toggle back to the appropriate settings.

Zoom does not have customer care, but it has an online FAQ section that is frequently updated to troubleshoot myriad issues. Specifically, visit https://support.zoom.us/hc/en-us/sections/200277708-Frequently-Asked-Questions. It is also suggested that your school administration engage in tech support as a part of its distance learning administration team—this may even be your school's technology teacher.

Zoom's most recent updates have also been extremely safety-focused with the onset of mass student use, to protect the privacy, data, and classrooms of educators and their students. Please make sure that you install new updates as they appear and have your class do the same. With each new update, test that Zoom is working before hosting your class, to see if you might need to try one of the quick fixes previously listed before starting your lecture.

Finally, as a last-ditch effort, if other educators across the board are noticing that Zoom isn't working, use your web browser to search for Zoom Outage Map. You may be in an area where Zoom is experiencing issues.

Part 3

Keeping Students Engaged/Classroom Management

As covered in Part 1, student engagement is the *key* metric in student success with distance learning. Finding ways to engage your students in lectures, materials, auxiliary resources, self-study, student discussions (both in breakout rooms and outside of class time), and group projects is the pathway to the greatest triumph in this format. The other key pillar of success to balance engagement, individualism, and creativity is structure. That can be created through impeccable classroom management.

While it might seem like a Herculean task to have the weight of both engagement and structure on your shoulders, there are a number of simple-to-employ tips that will make it seamless, and you might even find it's less of a burden than its in-person counterpart.

Administering Tests and Quizzes

Whether you are administering a short quiz or test during class time while on Zoom or having students take a test in out-of-class time via the school's online learning platform, the key administrative features of test tasking for distance learners are as follows.

1. Remind students of the school code of honor and ethics; have them promise not to cheat using other technological devices. Doing so dissuades the majority of students from engaging in unethical practice. Remind them again before every test and quiz.

2. For quizzes, focus on multiple-choice questions that can be auto-marked. You can add a touch of personalization to this by having a pop-up explain the correct answer or by sending out an answer key later.

3. Be sure that students are aware of the test time, and have them let you know in advance if they will not be able to make it. Be sure students know the time limit for each test. Be sure they know generally what will be covered on the test. Be firm and exacting with all of this information so students cannot find a way to misinterpret it. Send them an email with a document outlining this, especially for important tests.

4. Get back to students in a timely manner. Because they may continue to do poorly if they bombed the most recent test, it's important to address those issues ahead of the next one.

5. Figure out one way to administer tests, and stick to it. Either do it during class time or outside of it. Provide tests over the school's online learning portal or via a third-party server, like https://www.liveworksheets.com or Google Forms. Whatever it is, remain consistent so your test takers aren't foiled by new setups and new technology every time they take an exam.

The following are key ways to foster engagement in test taking.

1. Host a help session outside of normal school hours. Think of this as after-school time. Outside of your office hours, set aside an hour to do test prep with any interested students, to field their questions and to go over materials with them. Let students lead that session with their questions and their confusion, and make sure that every student who enters has time to ask at least one question. When a student asks a question, ask who else in the group has the same question, and use it as feedback for how many students you are helping at a time and what, if anything, a majority of students seemed unclear on in your lectures. This is a great way to engage, teacher to student, which is vitally important to success, especially for struggling students or students who just want a little more class time and face time with their peers and instructor. Since help sessions will likely not pull in the entire class, these can also be more intimate group sizes, allowing for people to be off mute and to chat and speak at will. Try to hold a poll during your Zoom class before any big tests to see what dates and times in the free spots on your calendar work best for students to come to a help session, and select the most popular one. Students who can't make it can always email you or catch you during office hours.

2. Arrange for study buddies. You can set up a study buddy system if your class is amenable to it. Students are typically better problem solvers in groups and pairs, and if you allow students to volunteer to be paired up with a study buddy, they can decide on their own times to pop onto Zoom and review materials together. Students tend to display and foster more advanced critical thinking skills and improved problem-solving when working together, and pairing students up may help fill in gaps or answer questions they didn't know they had. You can always offer a little extra incentive for groups that prove they did an hour's study buddy time before a test: a few extra bonus points, for example. This can be vital because engaging with their peers is just as important to students' education as engaging with you.

3. Provide personalized feedback. Tell students where and how they can improve, and praise what they do well. Instead of saying "This is right" or "This is wrong," give exact examples: "Your sentence structure was wonderful here, and I enjoyed your use of metaphor" versus "You used the wrong formula here. The correct formula for this kind of equation is ..." As much as your online platform allows, make their graded tests feel like a conversation more than a judgment.

4. Take time to go over the test, inside or out of class. Students who did poorly can't learn from their wrong answers, so take the time to go over tests and quizzes—especially questions many students got marked incorrect for. If the test would take too much class time to go over, host a test cool-down hour to review the material. Or you can always prerecord yourself going over each of the questions, and send that recording to your students. However, doing this live will produce more engagement and will lead to better clarity for your class.

5. Be willing to speak with parents. If parents want to have a meeting about an especially bad grade, be willing to speak with them about what can be done to improve those grades going forward. On the flip side, reach out to parents of students who have shown vast improvement or who are performing consistently well. This personalized praise can help bolster students' confidence and inspire them to work harder to have the kind of parent-teacher conference they definitely want.

Essays will function in much the same way. Provide personalized feedback, conduct help sessions beforehand, and take class time to read some of your favorite sample lines or paragraphs (anonymously) from students who performed well. For those who didn't, don't simply dock points and say "This is done poorly." Take the time to explain where it went right and how to improve the places it went wrong.

For many low-level quizzes, like quizzes about the lectures themselves, you can ask students to score themselves at the end of the class after reading out the answers. These will not count for actual grades but will be a good gauge for students of how much attention they were paying: either a nice surprise or a wake-up call to pay more attention.

Presentations that will be graded as tests should be done one-on-one or teacher to group, and you should find appropriate time slots within the class time to do these. This is especially important for foreign language discussion classes. You can give students a rough rubric of what you will be talking about or asking in advance, but make sure to switch up your topics and questions between students so they are unable to read from a script. You may even ask them to share their screen, if allowed by your school policies, if you suspect that they are reading from their notes in a presentation where this is not allowed. In the case where students are welcome to use notes, this is not a worry.

Assigning Homework

Homework in the distance learning world should be more open-ended than in the physical classroom—insofar as is possible. Try to make homework a less focused "task list," and instead give students options to explore your subject on their own terms. Instead of a single assignment, give an option between two or three. Because they spend so much of their distance learning life on-screen, being assigned hands-on homework can be extremely freeing or engaging for them.

In general, all homework will be submitted to you via your school's online learning portal. Some portals do not have restrictive time limits placed on students for submitting work. Despite that, make sure that your students are absolutely clear on what their homework assignments are, your expectations for them, and the *exact* date and time they are due. Even if they are able to submit work past that date and time, retain a sense of structure by letting them know it won't be accepted late without good reason and parental proof. Some online school platforms allow students to submit on a rolling basis, which means students can submit work very late and then complain when it does not count—some may even be missing time stamps. If students feel they need to be late submitting homework, encourage them to let you know that ahead of the due date—by more than five minutes.

If your school does not have an online portal with which to set up homework, you must use email to accept homework. Or you can have homework be presented live during class time to lead you into the next lecture and avoid submissions altogether—have it add to students' participation grades.

For students who will have technological difficulties submitting homework via email or an online portal, mail physical copies of homework to them. It is fine to mail these in bulk and to allow these students to submit the work at the end of each month or even semester, to save on money, time, and hassle. This unique situation must be accommodated, with no exceptions. Get to know your individual students' online capabilities and how they might affect their homework.

As ever, have a weekly set of dedicated office hours over Zoom during which students can come and ask you for homework help, among other things. Let students know, however, that if no one comes within the first five minutes of your Zoom office hours (and you don't receive an email or message from a student explaining that they will be arriving at a later time in that hour slot), you will leave office hours and resume your busy day.

Rather than get inundated with homework help questions, have office hours dedicated to this. If possible to aid in having fewer office hours, it may be better to assign weekly homework rather than daily homework, provide homework live online in bulk in advance, or allow for flexible homework problem-solving (such as letting students research any historical figure, rather than a specific one). This may cut back on the number of times students need to contact you for homework help and clarification outside of the classroom setting or office hours.

Determining Online Participation

Participation is important, especially in distance learning—but it's also especially tricky in that online space haunted by the Mute button and fraught with the fear of interrupting the teacher's scant lecture time, especially if those lectures also need to cover going over quizzes and homework, addressing group questions, doing group work in breakout rooms, and conducting morning meetings or closing circles.

Step one to encouraging participation is to take a deep breath. Because your notes and presentations and even your lectures may be digitized and prerecorded, it's okay if you don't get through everything. Facilitating discussion can be more important than forging ahead relentlessly.

To encourage participation and help students to get that grade, call on students frequently and by name, rather than asking a question and waiting to see who will answer. When two unmute at once, it can create stress and make shier students unwilling to do so. Calling by name can also be a sign to let students know they should remain focused on the lesson. If a student doesn't know an answer, don't shame them; call on someone else, and give them another try next lesson. If a student is able to reply with an insightful answer that proves they were paying attention, make a note of it on a physical attendance sheet or notebook, and add this to their participation grade. Rotate through students so everyone has a shot.

Do not typically use auxiliary time (office hours, study groups, pre-test question-and-answer sessions) to judge participation. This might cause you to inadvertently penalize students who understand the material well or who learn better on their own. Still, if someone who often cannot answer in class *does* participate in a fair amount of these extra-time classes, you might boost their participation grade—perhaps they interact better without the full class watching, and that's okay. It's all a part of the individualization that distance learning so excels at.

To help bolster participation grades, assign a different student an opening activity per class, such as sharing an interesting fact they learned while doing their homework or sharing an interesting quote from the reading. This can be a helpful way for students who are shier to accrue participation points; they may be reluctant to answer when put on the spot suddenly but able to shine if given time to prepare.

Plan group projects as well. Literally presenting a project to the class can count toward participation in a pretty evident way.

And remember, participation doesn't just have to be vocal. Outside of Zoom, it is likely that your school will have an online forum where students can ask questions, share resources, and chat. Keep an eye on this for participation as well.

In some cases, students with limited internet access or shaky Wi-Fi may simply not be able to participate as well as others. Again, be sure to be aware of your students' individual Wi-Fi and technological situations and to adjust your participation grades accordingly: a student should not be penalized for being *unable* to participate.

If your students are required to keep their cameras off during lessons and lectures, the same advice can be applied to vocal replies and presentations, even if you will not be able to *see* if your students are participating. You're a teacher; you'll know just by the sound of their "Huh?" if they weren't focused.

A last way to judge participation is to assign a multiple-choice quiz at the start of the class, with questions you will answer during the course of the lecture. High grades on these quizzes might result in a high participation grade. However, this method is the least foolproof, as students (especially off camera) can just Google answers at the start of class or share answers over private messaging at the end of class.

At the end of each lesson, again, give students vocal feedback. Tell participants who excelled that they did a good job, and tell students who did less well or could not answer not to worry, and you'll chat with them again next time. Extend and authenticate your students' participation in this way by acknowledging it.

Part 4

Activities and Sample Lesson Ideas

The truly exciting part of distance learning with Zoom is that the sky is the limit when it comes to ideas for activities. Technology is the opposite of limiting. This section covers a plethora of ideas for activities you can engage in to customize your classes to make them memorable, collaborative, and thoughtful.

Morning Meetings/Closing Circles

Your morning meeting (or afternoon meeting, depending on when you see your class) can help to set the tone of your lesson. It can pull students in, capture their focus, and center them for the lesson ahead. Try to come up with activities that complement the length and frequency of your lessons. If you see a class for an hour and a half every day, you can maybe have a 15-minute morning meeting, but if you see a class for an hour every other day, 5 minutes every other class might be more your speed. They can run as long as 20–30 minutes, however. It's up to your preference.

It's important to creating a sense of normalcy that you begin your classes with a structured greeting to warm students up, remind them of your personality, tell them it's time for YOUR class, and get the ball rolling to pull them into the correct headspace with an activity related to what you plan to do that day.

Here's how it works.

Say Hello!

Your morning meeting should start with a form of taking attendance and greeting all students by name with a "Hello, nice to see you" or "How are you?" as you go through the list. Personalizing this by adding little notes like "Oh, Adam, I'm looking forward to your presentation today!" or "Betty, are you feeling better from your cold?" can help students feel you have a real connection with them and that they matter. For classes where roll-call attendance is impossible or too unwieldly (25 or more students, for instance, which is certainly more common in higher learning spaces), just pick out a few people to name and address, switching it up each class.

Care and Share

If you're working with younger students, a great activity can be to ask them something empathetic but not too personal. For instance, you might go around the room and ask everyone how their weekend was, if they'd done anything exciting since they'd last seen you, if they'd learned anything cool, what their favorite moment lately was, or how they are feeling that day.

Feedback, as ever, is key. Don't just move on after Billy or Cynthia answers. Reply to what they've said, thoughtfully, and ask any follow-up questions you feel their story requires, such as "Oh, you watched a Disney movie? Do you have a favorite Disney character?" or "Was any part of the film especially funny?"

Show your interest, and they will repay your attention back to you when it's time to learn.

Group Action!

For older students, instead of sharing time, group activities work a little bit better. Think of upbeat activities that focus on members of the class working together and getting excited. You want to make sure that these activities not only sharpen their academic skills but also keep their social skills sharp. Some good examples are to have each person name their favorite food and have the next person in line name all of the favorite foods before them. You can also get physical: have students do a funny lip-synch to a song, recite poetry they like, play their guitar live, or act out short skits. The sky is the limit. But get them talking, and get them smiling.

You can also do activities that relate to or sum up your last lecture, especially if they had homework on it. Have them play an old Roman game, solve a tough but silly math problem as a group or in teams, or pretend to explain their last science experiment as an interesting figure (say, Bill Nye the Science Guy or Queen Victoria). Encourage silliness and creativity in this space.

Message in a Bottle

Finally, wrap up by taking the class back over and quieting all the excitement by imparting a message that will roll right into your lecture. Use a poem or a quote, or talk about how their activity relates to what they're about to learn. This can set the tone for the whole lecture, and it can also be the diving point between the fun of the morning meeting and the more serious academics of the class itself. It's a signal to quiet down and get more introspective after shaking the metaphorical cobwebs off their brains and limbs.

Closing Circles

If the morning meeting lets them siphon off energy, sharpen their social skills, and flex their critical thinking skills, entering the lesson refreshed, then the closing circle has much the same effect, but with more of a cooling tone than a warming tone. Just as in sports you need to stretch out before working out, then stretch out again to finish to prevent muscle stiffness, think of this as the second stretch that wards off long-class fatigue.

Introduction to Teaching with **Zoom**

For younger students, assign a certain gesture, like raising and flexing your hand, to signal that it's time for everyone to quiet down for closing circle. With older students, you can simply say that it's time for it.

Closing circles, while optional, can be vital to creating that elusive sense of consistency and routine for grades K–9. This is much less necessary for high school students, though it is a nice touch.

Closing circles should typically take no more than 10 minutes. As much as possible, encourage many, if not all, students to participate.

Close by asking the group a question in one of the following two categories:

- Introspective

- Festive

An example of an introspective question is:

- "What is one thing you learned today that you don't think your parents or relatives know, or that you could teach them later, or are excited to share with them?"

- Introspective questions allow students to think deeply and pause and take stock of what they've just learned, more firmly adjusting its place in their memory. It flexes their cognitive thinking.

An example of a festive question is:

- "What is one thing you did in class today, or that a fellow student did in class today, that you're really proud of, or thought was neat?"

- Festive questions make students feel positive about the learning experience, and as they look for just one thing to hone in on as worthy of praise that day, they're sharpening their deductive reasoning.

Growth Mindset Activity

A *growth mindset* activity takes a look at students' progress from *their* perspective. It is a list of investigative questions, often set up in a checkerboard design or some other design medium that feels engaging, that tracks where they feel they've improved the most and where they are worried they are lacking. It asks them if they are willing to continue improving in the face of roadblocks and impediments—the definition of a growth mindset is, in fact, overcoming hardship to improve, rather than smooth-sailing improvement. It teaches students that it's okay to have trouble, mess up, or even fail, so long as you can work together to come up with solutions on how they can try again and feel empowered to do better rather than demotivated by a lack of immediate success. Growth mindset is important for struggling students but equally for high-achieving students who may feel like a single bad grade or piece of constructive criticism has turned their world upside down. It teaches students to think of school life, and life in general, as an evolving journey rather than a series of harshly judged destinations and ranking orders. This way of thinking is even more vitally important during the uncertain times that lead to mass distance learning, like the COVID-19 pandemic, where nothing is "smooth sailing," and many students have lost touch with their everyday routines and had to adjust quite abruptly. This does not have to be destabilizing if it is turned into a collaborative learning moment that fosters new problem-solving abilities.

In contrast, the opposite of a growth mindset is a *fixed mindset*, describing students who are stuck, who feel their abilities are stagnant, or who think they cannot progress in class or excel beyond their current aptitudes. This can either be the sign of a student who is superciliously unaware that learning is a state of constantly improving or the sign of a student who is feeling gloomy, left behind, or inept.

Design your own growth mindset questions as a road map to help students examine the parts of themselves they may not have cast a keen eye on recently, and use their answers to help promote the positive aspects of a growth mindset: "What can I do to improve?" versus "I give up" or "I don't need improvement."

Some examples of growth mindset questions are:

- "Who do you feel will give you candid feedback about yourself? Who do you turn to for honest advice?"

- "If you felt you were struggling in class or in life, would you ask for help? Whom would you ask for help?"

- "What made the last task difficult for you, if it was? Or, if it was easy, what could you have done to test yourself more?"

- "What have you learned from a recent mistake you made? How will you change your strategy in the future?"

You can also pepper these into your lessons, as morning meeting or closing circle questions, if you do not want to assign them in bulk as a midsemester check-in.

Growth mindset activities can be employed at any time during a Zoom class but may be more interesting and helpful to assign as homework. Teachers can design their own growth mindset "mood boards" and share their screen live in class to go over each of the questions. However, since the probing questions in a mindset activity can be personal and sensitive, they are a prime way to take a temperature of how your students feel they are progressing, and so the answers might be more accurate and introspective if you allow students in grades 6–12 (and higher learning students) to sit with them and submit their answers to you privately. Therefore, for students in grade 6 and up, send your growth mindset activity via email or through the online learning portal after covering it in class, and have them submit to you their answers in text. To form that vital bond of engagement despite the use of text, assign this right before doing one-on-ones with your students about their own progress, and have them explain parts of their answers to you.

Even if you will cover these one-on-one over Zoom with individual students, make sure to provide supportive text feedback to their assignment right away.

For younger students, do growth mindset activities live and as a class. Younger students are slightly less guileless and more prone to sharing.

Building Community and Empathy

Ironically, as the world opens up through distance learning, local community becomes more important than ever. Empathy building is especially important for students who are socially isolated to help them feel connected with their peers, their town, and current events. Without activities built around empathy and community, students are liable to feel adrift in their distance learning. And we've all had that feeling that time has no meaning and place doesn't matter.

To reel students back in, get them engaged in empathy building!

Here are a few localized ideas to get you started:

1. Encourage lessons related to local good-news stories. Have students write essays or reports or give presentations on them. This will get them feeling good about their community and involved with local happenings.

2. Have students research a historic building or person in their area. Format an activity around that.

3. Have students handwrite or draw a thank-you letter to the workers who keep their day going. This could be their mail carrier, their local grocer, the mayor, or even their parents. Have them address and stamp the letter, even if the stamp is done in crayon and the address is "The A&P My Parents Like to Shop At" to give the letters that authentic feel. If they do not have envelopes, do an origami class on how to make them!

4. Have students plan a fundraiser for a local charity. Have them vote on the charity from a list you provide and then brainstorm ideas on how to help. Your local pet adoption center might thank you!

5. Emphasize "us and them," not "us versus them." Remember community through times of distance learning. Though local community is very important, now more than ever, so is global community. Creating empathy, especially in young people, can come from activities that show their lives are not so different from those of students in Japan, or Kenya, or Brazil. Have your students engage in cultural learning, and ask them: What do you think makes us the same? What are some differences that we could learn from, or celebrate?

Final Words

A friend of mine who teaches high school English literature summed up the difference between in-person learning and distance learning perfectly as she was tugged into the whirlwind of COVID-19 changes and her commute to school went from being an hour long to being a two-minute shuffle from the coffee machine in her kitchen to her desk:

"The main difference is that now I can look at everyone's work whenever I need to, rather than checking in on each student twice or three times per lesson like in a normal classroom environment. This is actually an advantage of distance learning—I have seen some students who had been distracted in my class produce much higher quality work when they had that quiet time alone at home and the personalized feedback. And the goals have shifted to really practicing and developing the students' skills rather than a race to teach new ones."

Of course, we want students to be ever learning and ever growing in our classrooms. But rather than thinking of distance learning as an unfortunate pause stymieing all of that, we have the opportunity to use amazing resources like Zoom to connect on a deeper level to our students and to encourage them more than ever before. Beyond Zoom, and supplementing it, there is a plethora of wonderful apps, websites, virtual tours, and supplementary lectures students otherwise never would have had access to—from free viewing of New York's Metropolitan Opera to the indulgence of at-home crafting and experimentation projects on DIY.org. Let's embrace distance learning and help craft its narrative for the best outcomes possible.

Happy Zooming!

About the Author

Madison Salters is a writer, editor, translator, and educator. She works for the online learning initiative Jolt as a lecturer on its global campuses for continuing education. Trained in using Zoom for education, she has also taught and tutored in ESL, foreign languages, and other subjects to K–12 students both in the United States and in France. She lives in New York City.